BASKET

BASIN

PLATE

AND CUP

VESSELS IN THE LITURGY

Edited by David Philippart

LTP

LITURGY
TRAINING
PUBLICATIONS

dgments

... the *New Revised Standard Version of the Bible* © 1989 Division
... he National Council of Churches of Christ in the United States.
... *vironment and Art in Catholic Worship* © 1978 United States Catholic
... SCC), Washington, D.C. Used with permission. All rights reserved. No
... ment may be reproduced by any means without permission in writing from
... owner. "Order for the Blessing of a Chalice and Paten" from the *Book of*
... additional blessings for use in the United States of America © 1988 USCC. Used
... permission. All rights reserved. No portion of this work may be reproduced by any means
...ithout permission in writing from the copyright owner.

The English translation of the "Blessing of a Chalice and a Paten" from the *Dedication of a Church and an Altar* © 1978 International Committee on English in the Liturgy, Inc. (ICEL); excerpts from the English translation of *Documents on the Liturgy, 1963–1979: Conciliar, Papal, and Curial Texts* © 1982 ICEL. All rights reserved.

"Dedication of Worship Furnishings" from *The Lutheran Book of Worship* is reprinted from Occasional Services © 1982 by permission of Augsburg Fortress.

The quote on pages 43–44 from Theophilus is taken from *On Divers Arts: The Foremost Medieval Treatise on Painting, Glassmaking and Metalwork*, translated by John G. Hawthorne and Cyril Stanley Smith (New York: Dover Publications, 1979), pages 77–80. Used with permission.

"For a Holy Purpose" by Edward Foley began as a paper published in the *1991 Proceedings of the North American Academy of Liturgy*, which was revised and published in the June 1992 issue of *Environment & Art Letter*. It has been further revised by the author for inclusion in this book. The following chapters all first appeared as articles in the indicated issues of *Environment & Art Letter*, LTP's monthly magazine on church architecture and art, edited by David Philippart: "Thinking about Vessels" by Mark Humenick (April 1996); "Thoughts on Ambries and the Oil Stocks" by Peter Mazar (November 1996); "Thuribles" by Gregory Yoshida (December 1990); "Caring for Metalware" by Marirose Jelicich (March 1991). To order a subscription to *Environment & Art Letter*, call 1-800-933-1800.

"Liturgical Vessels Today" is adapted from chapter 21 of *The Sacristy Manual* by G. Thomas Ryan (Chicago: LTP, 1992).

BASKET, BASIN, PLATE AND CUP: VESSELS IN THE LITURGY © 2001 Archdiocese of Chicago: Liturgy Training Publications, 1800 North Hermitage Avenue, Chicago IL 60622-1101; 1-800-933-1800; fax 1-800-933-7094; orders@ltp.org. All rights reserved.

Visit our website at www.ltp.org.

This book was designed by Larry Cope, typeset in Caslon and Matrix by Karen Mitchell, and printed by Palace Press International in Hong Kong. It was conceived, compiled and edited by David Philippart. Bryan Cones was the production editor.

Printed in China.

05 04 03 02 01   5 4 3 2 1

Library of Congress Cataloging-in-Publication Data
Basket, basin, plate and cup : vessels in the liturgy / edited by David Philippart.
     p. cm.
    ISBN 1-56854-190-2 (pbk.)
   1. Catholic Church—Liturgical objects. 2. Catholic Church—Doctrines. I. Philippart, David.
BX1925 .N37 2001
247—dc21
                                         00-052014

BASKET

Pass the basket.

Pour the pitcher.

Fill the basin.

Empty the bowl.

Lift the plate.

Raise the cup.

Give God thanks and praise,

thanks and praise.

ents

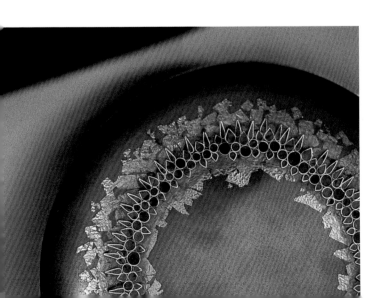

I

All These Vessels

BEZALEL MADE

Bezalel made the ark of acacia wood; it was two and a half cubits long, a cubit and a half wide, and a cubit and a half high. He overlaid it with pure gold inside and outside, and made a molding of gold around it. He cast for it four rings of gold for its four feet, two rings on its one side and two rings on its other side. He made poles of acacia wood, and overlaid them with gold, and put the poles into the rings on the sides of the ark, to carry the ark. He made a mercy seat of pure gold; two cubits and a half was its length, and a cubit and a half its width. He made two cherubim of hammered gold; at the two ends of the mercy seat he made them, one cherub at the one end, and one cherub at the other end; of one piece with the mercy seat he made the cherubim at its two ends. The cherubim spread out their wings above, overshadowing the mercy seat with their wings. They faced one another; the faces of the cherubim were turned toward the mercy seat.

He also made the table of acacia wood, two cubits long, one cubit wide, and a cubit and a half high. And he made the vessels of pure gold that were to be on the table, its plates and dishes for incense, and its bowls and flagons with which to pour drink offerings.

He also made the lampstand of pure gold. The base and the shaft of the lampstand were made of hammered work; its cups, its calyxes, and its petals were of one piece with it. There were six branches going out of its sides, three branches of the lampstand out of one side of it and three branches of the lampstand out of the other side of it; three cups shaped like almond blossoms, each with calyx and petals, on one branch, and three cups shaped like almond blossoms, each with calyx and petals, on the other branch—so for the six branches going out of the lampstand. Their calyxes and their branches were of one piece with it, the whole of it one hammered piece of pure gold. He made its seven lamps and its snuffers and its trays of pure gold. He made it and all its utensils of a talent of pure gold.

He made all the utensils of the altar, the pots, the shovels, the basins, the forks, and the firepans: all its utensils he made of bronze.

He made the basin of bronze with its stand of bronze, from the mirrors of the women who served at the entrance to the tent of meeting.

Exodus 37:1–10, 16–19, 22–24; 38:3, 8

TWELVE PLATES

This was the dedication offering for the altar, at the time when it was anointed, from the leaders of Israel: twelve silver plates, twelve silver basins, twelve gold dishes.

Numbers 7:84

ALL THESE VESSELS

Now King Solomon invited and received Hiram from Tyre. He was the son of a widow of the tribe of Naphtali, whose father, a man of Tyre, had been an artisan in bronze; he was full of skill, intelligence, and knowledge in working bronze. He came to King Solomon, and did all his work.

The pots, the shovels, and the basins, all these vessels that Hiram made for King Solomon for the house of the LORD were of burnished bronze. In the plain of the Jordan the king cast them, in the clay ground between Succoth and Zarethan.

So Solomon made all the vessels that were in the house of the LORD: the golden altar, the golden table for the bread of the Presence, the lampstands of pure gold, five on the south side and five on the north, in front of the inner sanctuary; the flowers, the lamps, and the tongs, of gold; the cups, snuffers, basins, dishes for incense, and firepans, of pure gold; the sockets for the doors of the innermost part of the house, the most holy place, and for the doors of the nave of the temple, of gold.

Thus all the work that King Solomon did on the house of the LORD was finished. Solomon brought in the things that his father David had dedicated, the silver, the gold, and the vessels, and stored them in the treasuries of the house of the LORD.

1 Kings 7:13–14, 45–46, 48–51

BASKET OF UNLEAVENED BREAD

The LORD said to Moses, "You shall also take the fat of the ram, the fat tail, the fat that covers the entrails, the appendage of the liver, the two kidneys with the fat that is on them, and the right thigh (for it is the ram of ordination), and one loaf of bread, one cake of bread made with oil, and one wafer, out of the basket of unleavened bread that is before the LORD; and you shall place all these on the palms of Aaron and on the palms of his sons, and raise them as an elevation offering before the LORD.

Exodus 29:22–24

THEY FILLED TWELVE BASKETS

Jesus went to the other side of the Sea of Galilee, also called the Sea of Tiberias. A large crowd kept following him, because they saw the signs that he was doing for the sick. Jesus went up the mountain and sat down there with his disciples. Now the Passover, the festival of the Jews, was near. When he looked up and saw a large crowd coming toward him, Jesus said to Philip, "Where are we to buy bread for these people to eat?" He said this to test him, for he himself knew what he was going to do. Philip answered him, "Six months' wages would not buy enough bread for each of them to get a little." One of his disciples, Andrew, Simon Peter's brother, said to him, "There is a boy here who has five barley loaves and two fish. But what are they among so many people?"

Jesus said, "Make the people sit down." Now there was a great deal of grass in the place; so they sat down, about five thousand in all. Then Jesus took the loaves, and when he had given thanks, he distributed them to those who were seated; so also the fish, as much as they wanted.

When they were satisfied, he told his disciples, "Gather up the fragments left over, so that nothing may be lost." So they gathered them up, and from the fragments of the five barley loaves, left by those who had eaten, they filled twelve baskets. When the people saw the sign that he had done, they began to say, "This is indeed the prophet who is to come into the world."

John 6:1–14

A PAPYRUS BASKET

Pharoah commanded all his people, "Every boy that is born to the Hebrews you shall throw into the Nile, but you shall let every girl live."

Now a man from the house of Levi went and married a Levite woman. The woman conceived and bore a son; and when she saw that he was fine baby, she hid him three months. When she could hide him no longer she got a papyrus basket for him, and plastered it with bitumen and pitch; she put the child in it and placed it among the reeds on the bank of the river. His sister stood at a distance, to see what would happen to him.

The daughter of Pharoah came down to bathe at the river, while her attendants walked beside the river. She saw the basket among the reeds and sent her maid to bring it. When she opened it, she saw the child. He was crying, and she took pity on him.

Exodus 1:22—2:6

OVER THE WALL IN A BASKET

After some time had passed, the authorities plotted to kill Saul, but their plot became known to him. They were watching the gates day and night so that they might kill him; but his disciples took him by night and let him down through an opening in the wall, lowering him in a basket.

Acts of the Apostles 9:23–25

SIX STONE JARS OF WATER INTO WINE

On the third day there was a wedding in Cana of Galilee, and the mother of Jesus was there. Jesus and his disciples had also been invited to the wedding. When the wine gave out, the mother of Jesus said to him, "They have no more wine." And Jesus said to her, "Woman, what concern is that to you and to me? My hour has not yet come." His mother said to the servants, "Do whatever he tells you." Now standing there were six stone water jars for the Jewish rites of purification, each holding twenty or thirty gallons. Jesus said to them, "Fill the jars with water." And they filled them up to the brim. He said to them, "Now draw some out, and take it to the chief steward." So they took it. When the steward tasted the water that had become wine, and did not know where it came from (though the servants who had drawn the water knew), the steward called the bridegroom and said to him, "Everyone serves the good wine first, and then the inferior wine after the guests have become drunk. But you have kept the good wine until now."

Jesus did this, the first of his signs, in Cana of Galilee, and revealed his glory; and his disciples believed in him.

John 2:1–11

CARRYING A WATER JAR

On the first day of Unleavened Bread, when the Passover lamb is sacrificed, Jesus' disciples said to him, "Where do you want us to go and make the preparations for you to eat the Passover?" So he sent two of his disciples, saying to them, "Go into the city, and a man carrying a jar of water will meet you; follow him, and wherever he enters, say to the owner of the house, 'The Teacher asks, Where is my guest room where I may eat the Passover with my disciples?' He will show you a large room upstairs, furnished and ready. Make preparations for us there." So the disciples set out and went to the city, and found everything as he had told them; and they prepared the Passover meal.

Mark 14:12–16

AN ALABASTER JAR

While Jesus was at Bethany in the house of Simon the leper, as he sat at the table, a woman came in with an alabaster jar of very costly ointment of nard, and she broke open the jar and poured the ointment on his head. But some were there who said to one another in anger, "Why was the ointment wasted in this way? For this ointment could have been sold for more than three hundred denarii, and the money given to the poor." And they scolded her. But Jesus said, "Let her alone; why do you trouble her? She has performed a good service for me. For you always have the poor with you, and you can show kindness to them whenever you wish; but you will not always have me. She has done what she could; she has anointed my body beforehand for its burial. Truly I tell you, wherever the good news is proclaimed in the whole world, what she has done will be told in remembrance of her."

Mark 14:3–9

WATER IN A BASIN

Then Jesus poured water into a basin and began to wash the disciples' feet and to wipe them with the towel that was tied around him.

John 13:5

HE TOOK A CUP

While they were eating, Jesus took a loaf of bread, and after blessing it he broke it, gave it to them, and said, "Take; this is my body." Then he took a cup, and after giving thanks he gave it to them, and all of them drank from it. He said to them, "This is my blood of the covenant, which is poured out for many. Truly I tell you, I will never again drink of the fruit of the vine until that day when I drink it new in the kingdom of God."

Mark 14:22–25

REMOVE THIS CUP

They went to a place called Gethsemane; and he said to his disciples, "Sit here while I pray." He took with him Peter and James and John, and began to be distressed and agitated. And he said to them, "I am deeply grieved, even to death; remain here and keep awake." And going a little farther, he threw himself on the ground and prayed that, if it were possible, the hour might pass from him. He said, "Abba, Father, for you all things are possible; remove this cup from me; yet, not what I want, but what you want."

Mark 14:32–36

THE CUP GIVEN ME

Then Simon Peter, who had a sword, drew it, struck the high priest's slave, and cut off his right ear. The slave's name was Malchus. Jesus said to Peter, "Put your sword back into its sheath. Am I not to drink the cup that the Father has given me?"

John 18:10–11

CHOSEN CUP

> The LORD is my chosen portion and my cup;
>
> you hold my lot.

Psalm 16:5

A JAR OF SOUR WINE

When Jesus knew that all was now finished, he said (in order to fulfill the scripture), "I am thirsty." A jar full of sour wine was standing there. So they put a sponge full of the wine on a branch of hyssop and held it to his mouth. When Jesus had received the wine he said, "It is finished." Then he bowed his head and delivered up his spirit.

John 19:28–30

CUP OF BLESSING

The cup of blessing that we bless, is it not a sharing in the blood of Christ? The bread that we break, is it not a sharing in the body of Christ? Because there is one bread, we who are many are one body, for we all partake of the one bread.

1 Corinthians 10:16–17

LIFT UP THE CUP

> What shall I return to the LORD
>> for all his bounty to me?
> I will lift up the cup of salvation
>> and call on the name of the LORD,
> I will pay my vows to the LORD
>> in the presence of all his people.

Psalm 116:12–14

DRINK THE CUP

For as often as you eat this bread and drink the cup, you proclaim the Lord's death until he comes.

1 Corinthians 11:26

CUP OF JUSTICE

Jesus said to his disciples, "Truly I tell you, whoever gives you a cup of water to drink because you bear the name of Christ will by no means lose the reward."

Mark 9:41

2

For a Holy Purpose

A HISTORICAL SURVEY OF VESSELS FOR LITURGY

Edward Foley, Capuchin

In one sense, Christianity was born around the domestic table. The meal traditions of Israel and the instinct to bless God always at the breaking of the bread provide the context in which specific Christian rituals emerged. Judaism had few vessels that it considered sacred in the execution of domestic rites. Similarly, the vessels of first-century Christianity were of a decidedly nonsacred nature. A cup, a pitcher, a basket served the bread and wine, which in turn served the unity of the assembly. Here it is not the things—not even the bread and the wine—that are important, but the community. The believers, more than any single food, are truly the body of Christ. For most of Christianity's first century, we are unable to discern clearly what we might call a Christian liturgy and, therefore, specific liturgical vessels. We only know that Christians ritualized and that they employed domestic vessels in that ritual.

Illustration 1

Roman drinking glass (first to second century CE).

Individual drinking cups were a familiar commodity in Jewish society, though it is not likely that individual cups were available to all the family members or guests at a meal. A communal cup was frequently used. A cup for ordinary use often was made of clay, though precious metals were used for goblets for the wealthy. During the first century, glass was a common material for cups in the Hellenistic world. Simple glass beakers and bowls with or without a base served as drinking vessels. Very seldom would a stem or node separate the base from the bowl. A simple glass cup is probably the kind of vessel Jesus used during the various ritual meals in which he participated, including the Last Supper (Illustration 1).

In the second and third centuries, the vessels for eucharist continued to be of a domestic quality. A wicker basket and a wooden bowl would have sufficed in many situations. Fragments of gold-glass from the catacombs of the period suggest that glass dishes were used as well. Because homes of the very wealthy were also used by the Christian community during this time, it is probable that assemblies also used precious goblets and trays of silver or gold. As Christian ritual vessels developed, precious metals were increasingly used for their fabrication. The tradition of fashioning eucharistic cups from precious metals seems to have been firmly established by the third century. This does not suggest, however, that gold and silver were used exclusively. There is evidence that glass, stone (including onyx), wood and bone were used to make eucharistic vessels up to the Middle Ages.

As to the size and shape of the eucharistic cups of this time, we can be sure that a single cup was ordinarily used during the eucharist. The size of such a cup would have been in proportion to the number of believers who gathered for worship. Given the capacity of some of the house churches of this era, this could have meant chalices large enough to serve 100 people or more. Some of the smaller gatherings could have employed a simple, stemless cup or even a bowl. The vessels reflected the size, the means and the needs of the community. In this era, therefore, we seem to have begun the move from domestic ritual vessels (vessels simply employed in the rituals of Christian life) to liturgical vessels (vessels fabricated for Christian liturgy and employed for no other purpose).

FROM DOMESTIC TO LITURGICAL VESSELS

Between the fourth and the seventh centuries significant changes occurred regarding the size and quality of liturgical vessels. What is most striking is the complete transition from household utensils to liturgical vessels. Wicker, clay and wood vessels were less commonly used, replaced most often by gold and silver. The large numbers that filled the Christian basilicas after the conversion of Constantine (312) made demands on the size of vessels for communion.

Illustration 2

A two-handled drinking cup from the pre-Constantinian Roman empire.

Since the earliest times, the symbolism of one bread and one cup required that there be one cup sufficiently large to hold wine for the whole community. Often these chalices were large, vase-shaped vessels attached to a round base. Handles were often attached to the side to aid in drinking (Illustration 2). We have examples of much smaller chalices from this period as well. The range in size does not indicate whether or not an assembly was communicating from the cup; rather, it indicates the size of the community.

In the early Middle Ages (the eighth to the eleventh centuries), eucharistic vessels underwent a reduction in their capacity. This was partly due to the change in the type of bread used. After the ninth century, unleavened bread became customary and eventually mandatory in the West. Patens that formerly were large enough to hold a loaf of bread became smaller. The bread to be distributed to the assembly was now held in a pyx, so the paten needed to be only large enough to hold the priest's host. Thus the concave disk, small enough to rest on top of the chalice, had already appeared by the tenth century.

Chalices of the period were smaller than those of the previous era. Reasons for the miniaturization of this vessel included a decline in the communion of the laity and the prevalence of the private Mass. Even when laity did receive communion, it seldom included drinking from the cup for fear that the precious blood would be spilled. The shape of the chalice changed further with the growing custom of separating the base from the cup with a node on the stem of the chalice (Illustration 3). This design, which helped the priest hold the chalice, was eventually mandated by church law.

Illustration 3

An eighth-century chalice with a small node.

Legislation concerning the material for fabricating chalices first appeared during this period. Initially, certain materials were disallowed: The Synod of Calechyt in 787, for example, outlawed the use of animal horn. Eventually, directives required that the chalice be made from gold or silver, although exceptions for poorer churches were allowed. As chalices came to be forged from precious metals and held beyond the reach of the laity, their sacrality was underscored by new rites of consecration that appeared at this time.

These phenomena indicate the development of the eucharistic theology of the period. Increasingly, the teaching of the church focused on the presence of Christ localized in the bread and the wine. This emphasis largely ignored the other modes of Christ's presence, especially in the assembly. To a certain extent, then, the vessels that held the sacred species became more precious than the community itself. Vessels were consecrated; people were increasingly restricted from communicating. Bread was no longer put in their hands but on their tongues. Drinking through a tube replaced drinking from the cup, and eventually the cup was completely withdrawn from the laity. These developments finalized the movement from liturgical vessels to truly sacred vessels, that is, vessels that were considered holy apart from their usage—so holy that even outside of worship only certain people could touch them.

FROM LITURGICAL TO SACRED VESSELS

From the twelfth to the fifteenth centuries, the vessels of the period reflected a growing preoccupation with the bread. By the eleventh century, the use of

unleavened bread was universal in the West. So was the practice of baking hosts of two different sizes, a larger one for the priest and smaller ones for the laity. Two-handled chalices disappeared in the late Middle Ages, along with communion from the cup by the laity. The cup was now often cone-shaped, attached to a hexagonal or octagonal stem. The node was often enameled, carved with images or even shaped into an elaborate architectural design, reflecting the style of the surrounding building. Bells were added to some chalices, possibly to highlight their elevation (Illustration 4).

Illustration 4

Chalice, showing Gothic architectural design influence, with bells.

More important was the emergence of vessels for the display of the host. As vessels for the containment and display of the bread increased, the number of vessels or utensils for the wine decreased. The laity had already ceased receiving from the cup. Now receiving the bread was perceived as being dangerous and became so infrequent that the church had to mandate yearly reception (1215). Seeing the bread became the ultimate substitute for eating it. What could no longer be touched with the hand was touched by sight, and seeing the host became sufficient for sustenance and salvation.

Though some changes in vessels occurred after the sixteenth-century Protestant Reformation, for Roman Catholics, at least, the Reformation era was not one of communion and communion vessels. Roman Catholics preferred to watch the elements, and communion remained an infrequent event. Much of the artistic development in Roman Catholic vessels during the post-Tridentine era concerned vessels that had nothing to do with the communion of the faithful. Only the priest received the wine, thus the elaboration of his chalice. The removal of the cup from the laity in the previous era contributed to the standardization of the chalice's shape and proportion (it often held only a few drops of wine and water for the priest). Further artistic elaboration had no real ritual function. Frequently, chalices and monstrances in the post-Tridentine era assumed baroque forms that mimicked the ecclesiastical architecture of the period. The conical cup, so popular in the Gothic era, was often abandoned for a rounded, bell- or tulip-shaped cup. Angular stems with a single node and geometric base gave way to rounded

Illustration 5

Left, a fourteenth-century monstrance. Right, a baroque monstrance from Klosterneuburg, Germany (1712–14 CE).

stems, a gently defined node often melding into two or three smaller nodes, terminating in a mound-like base. Monstrances also embodied the architecture of post-Tridentine churches. Rather than the static and symmetrical monstrances of the Gothic or Renaissance periods, baroque monstrances were often adorned with rays of precious metal emanating from the host (Illustration 5).

The early-twentieth-century tendency to reject ornamentation and artificiality in architecture affected the design of eucharistic vessels. The middle of the twentieth century eventually saw the emergence of vessels that eschewed ornamentation. The results were often sleek, contemporary works of art. This was sometimes achieved with traditional materials of silver and gold. Other times, however, new materials such as stainless steel were used.

A RETURN TO LITURGICAL VESSELS

A hallmark of the twentieth-century liturgical movement has been renewed belief in the centrality of the assembly in public worship. The evolution of eucharistic vessels in this century attests to the church's growing awareness of this. Vessels are not sacred because of the beauty of their design or the preciousness of their materials. Rather, they are sacred because they mediate presence to the assembly. And it is in the hands of the assembly that they belong.

This is a retreat from the notion of the sacred vessel and a return to the notion of the liturgical vessel. The return to full, rich symbols—bread that can be perceived as bread, for example (see the *General Instruction of the Roman Missal*, 283)—presumes that vessels are shaped accordingly. Sharing the cup within this richer symbolic framework means that wine should be drunk by all from a common vessel. The move toward more authentic symbols also effected a change in the materials used for eucharistic vessels. Though gold and silver continue to be employed, they are often replaced by glass, clay and wood. Even the use of wicker baskets for the eucharistic bread, reminiscent of primitive Christian worship, has been restored in some places.

THE MINISTERIAL STANDARD

Today we are returning to an ancient perspective and an authentically liturgical one. In this perspective, liturgical vessels do not inhabit a higher realm of being. Consequently, liturgical vessels cannot be judged apart from their ministerial function—their use to mediate divine presence to the assembly. This ministerial function has to be an integral consideration in the process of crafting and selecting vessels for use in worship.

Some might suggest that this functionalist approach leads us to second-class art. Because it requires taking into account the tastes and needs of the people of our assemblies, some complain that it reduces art to the lowest common denominator. As I have argued in other places, however, concerns about beauty and esthetics are themselves "functional concerns," albeit seldom acknowledged ones (see my "The Ritual-Musical Function of Music: From Assisi to Snowbird," *Pastoral Music* 21:3 [1997], 17–21).

The ministerial standard makes real demands on artists who are invited to direct their craft to a holy purpose. And that holy purpose is the praise of God through the sanctification of people. Liturgy is not simple praise of God, but praise of God through human beings called to become living praise. In the words of an ancient liturgical axiom, sacraments are for people, people are not for sacraments.

FUNCTIONAL ART

For liturgical musicians the ministerial standard means not only crafting beautiful music but also beautiful music that assemblies can actually sing; for architects it means not only creating breathtaking environments but also environments hospitable to human praise and interaction. And for those who shape liturgical vessels, it means shaping vessels that serve the Christian community, which is itself the true vessel of the presence of Christ.

Fundamentally, we need to ask if our liturgical vessels invite the eating and drinking at the heart of the Christian mystery or if they simply invite watching? Does the cup dazzle us, or does it invite us to pick it up? If this a beauty beyond our reach, does it suggest that the presence of Christ is equally beyond our reach? Does the vessel become the medium of something else, or does it become itself the primary message?

Here the principles for evaluation outlined in paragraphs 19 through 23 of *Environment and Art in Catholic Worship* (EACW) are most useful. The document notes that the two demands that liturgy makes on the arts are quality and appropriateness. Quality, according to the document, means "love and care in the making of something, honesty and genuineness with any materials used, and the artist's special gift in producing a harmonious whole, a well-crafted work" (#20). Appropriateness means that the artifacts must be "capable of bearing the weight of mystery, awe, reverence, and wonder which the liturgical action expresses," and "it must clearly *serve* (and not interrupt) [the] ritual action" (#21).

Specifically with regard to liturgical vessels, this means attention to materials, design and scale. In materials, as EACW notes, a ministerial standard "rules out anything trivial and self-centered, anything fake, cheap or shoddy, anything pretentious or superficial" (#22). Design, maybe even more than material, is the key cultural issue. Designing liturgical vessels according to a ministerial standard means shaping artifacts contiguous with the experiences and expectations of a given people at a specific time and place, that at the same time calls them to a place they've never been before. Finally, scale admits that liturgy is a human activity, a human activity not centered on the individual but owned and centered in a community.

In the movie *Witness* an urban detective seeks refuge in an Amish community, where he is also trying to protect a boy who witnessed a murder. The detective has brought a handgun into the Amish household in which he is staying. There is a scene where the handgun sits on the kitchen table while the grandfather tries to explain to his young grandson why guns are so bad. He makes a single, stunning observation. "My boy," he says, "what you put in your hand, you put in your heart." Let this be our guide as we take up human crafts for a holy purpose.

3

Vessels in the Liturgy Today

G. Thomas Ryan

SACRED AND ARTISTIC CONTAINERS

Reverence through the Ages

The vessels used at Christian liturgy have always reflected the importance of sacramental actions. As with our Jewish ancestors and neighbors, and with adherents to most other religions of the world, we set aside vessels for liturgical use that are distinguished by their size, form, nobility and decoration. Reformers and fundamentalists, today as in past epochs, prefer to see an antagonism between art and religion. Jews often are assumed to be anti-art because they are anti-idol. Some say that Christians are at their holiest and most "spiritual" when they have no need of art. Yet both Jewish and Christian history demonstrates that such opinions have never prevailed for long. The artifacts of every century show that liturgical communities have sought to bring their faith to expression with the most beautiful art and materials obtainable.

The sanctuary artisan Bezalel is praised in Exodus (35:30–33) as so filled with divine spirit that he was able to devise artistic designs, cut stones, carve wood and work in gold, silver and bronze. Later, in the 1,100 years between the construction of the first Jewish temple and the destruction of the last in about 70 CE, all Jews—including the disciples of Jesus—revered their holy place in Jerusalem, a building complex constructed of the finest materials and filled with precious vessels and artifacts. In later centuries, domestic and synagogue gatherings of Jews utilized wondrous plates and cups, lamp stands and spice boxes. Christians, too, in domestic prayer and in public liturgical assemblies, always used splendid liturgical vessels made by artists and artisans—their own Bezalels.

By the high Middle Ages, the separation of the liturgical action from the assembly, the clericalization of Christian communities, and numerous cultural forces had led to new understandings of liturgical elements. The presence of Christ in the bread and wine was understood in radically physical ways. At the same time, appreciation of the other modes of presence—in the community and God's word especially—was minimized. Priests were understood to be privileged because they consecrated the elements and could touch them, not because they were pastoral ministers or liturgical presiders in communion with those gathered. Vessels were cherished and held sacred more because they held Jesus rather than because they shaped the liturgical actions of sacred communities.

The *General Instruction of the Roman Missal* (#289–96) employs the term "sacred" to describe liturgical vessels, especially chalices and patens. Because of their centrality at our most revered and constitutive gatherings, because they "touch the Lord," Christian communities continue to esteem them and hold them sacred. Our respect and careful handling of chalices and patens, however, should not become so exaggerated or exclusive that we diminish respect for other vessels, such as those for holy oils or baptismal water. It's only natural that the most central vessels, the chalices and the patens, will continue to be created with more artistry than others. Yet all our vessels should be considered beautiful and holy, and handled accordingly, for they invite us to divine interaction.

Current Materials and Forms

The chalice and paten placed on the altar before the eucharistic prayer should each be large enough to attract the community's attention and to hold all of the bread or wine. The ideal of "one bread and one cup" has once more been enshrined in our liturgical norms (see, for example, *General Instruction of the Roman Missal*, 293; *Environment and Art in Catholic Worship*, 96). Other vessels should be designed and chosen to accommodate today's larger loaves of bread and more plentiful use of wine. These would include flagons to hold any wine that does not fit in the one cup, the many cups and plates into which the eucharistic meal is divided prior to distribution, pyxes, and cruets or pitchers.

The materials used should be solid, with preference given to those that do not break easily. They should be considered noble, "prized" in the community that uses them. And, of course, form should follow function. For example, a chalice should be lined with nonabsorbent material. As long as these vessels function appropriately in the liturgy, they can be made by artists in whatever shapes express the local community's faith. This suggests that local artists— not catalogs of mass-produced items—be consulted when vessels are needed.

WINE AND VESSELS FOR WINE

The Meanings of Cup-Sharing

Eucharistic cup-sharing was so essential to the act of sharing communion that, for early Christians, communion under the form of bread alone was truly rare. Communion from the cup was the sharing that formed ecclesial unity and reconciliation (1 Corinthians 10:16). It was wine mixed with a little water, like the mixtures shared even today in Mediterranean cultures, but more importantly, like the Sabbath cup of the Jews, a beverage of blessing and praise of God. It was perceived by communicants as a sharing of life and immortality. To drink of the cup was to express commitment to God's will. Its redness enhanced the sense of sharing blood, its alcoholic content was associated with the stimulation or conversion of human spirits and "spiritual inebriation."

In the Middle Ages, as part of the overall devolution of liturgical forms during that period, the eucharistic wine became reserved to the priest celebrant. Theologians maintained the rich meanings associated with eucharistic wine and the chalice, but the vitality of these meanings was compromised as the practice was curtailed. When reformers pressed for the restoration of cup-sharing to the assembly, Catholic bishops responded with the doctrine of concomitance—the belief that the whole Christ is received under either form of the eucharist; thus, the sharing of the chalice was not necessary for additional grace.

In the decades leading to Vatican II, pastoral liturgists recognized the deficiency of this perspective; communion offered under the form of bread alone ignored the integrity of the sacramental sign of bread and wine, and even violated the Lord's command to "take and drink." When the reforms of the council came, officials were concerned about explaining how sharing the cup could have been forbidden for so long and now encouraged, and how the doctrine of concomitance was not in question here. The Constitution on the Sacred Liturgy *Sacrosanctum concilium* treats this issue by noting that "[t]he dogmatic principles about the communion of the faithful which were laid down by the Council of Trent are confirmed, yet communion under both kinds may be granted when the bishops think fit, not only to clerics and religious but also to the laity, in cases to be determined by the Apostolic See" (#55).

A few years later, the instruction *Eucharisticum mysterium* continued the implementation and expounded its rationale:

> Holy communion has a more complete form as a sign when it is received under both kinds. For in this manner of reception (without prejudice to the principles laid down by the Council of Trent, that under each element Christ whole and entire and the true sacrament are received), a fuller light shines on the sign of the eucharistic banquet. Moreover there is a clearer expression of that will by which the new and everlasting covenant is ratified in the

blood of the Lord and of the relationship of the eucharistic banquet to the eschatological banquet in the Father's kingdom. (#32)

This elaboration of meanings found its way into the *General Instruction of the Roman Missal* (#240). As cup-sharing is practiced by more and more assemblies, as catechists and pastors fearlessly face the doubts about hygiene, these visions of covenant and banquet will more and more become part of common consciousness.

Wine

From time to time, there have been reformers intent on eliminating wine from the eucharist. From the second to the fifth centuries, ascetical groups (termed "Aquarians") refused to acknowledge that the messianic era symbolized by wine had been inaugurated with Jesus. They used water instead of wine and were fought vigorously by church leaders. Church councils similarly confronted another aberration, the substitution of milk for wine in seventh-century Spain. During the experiments of the 1960s, certain groups tried using elements other than bread and wine ("to be relevant"). Even today, certain Baptists and other Protestant churches use grape juice instead of wine. Despite all this, Catholic liturgical traditions have prevailed. Wine has survived as a vital sacramental sign, proclaiming the covenant, the messianic era and the spiritual inebriation of conversion.

The *General Instruction of the Roman Missal* (#284–85) sets the requirement for wine in brief terms: "The wine for the eucharist must be from the fruit of the vine (see Luke 22:18), natural, and pure, that is not mixed with any foreign substance. Care must be taken to ensure that the elements are kept in good condition: that the wine does not turn to vinegar."

Sacristans might periodically review their methods of storing and replenishing wine supplies. A good reserve is always appropriate, especially where large funerals can come at a moment's notice. Yet the supply should not be so great that any given bottle is kept for more than six months. For open bottles of wine, a small refrigerator helps preserve its taste.

The wine can be made by parish members (in those few geographic regions where this ideal is possible), donated by members, or purchased from any reputable supplier. Church goods stores and "sacramental wine" distributors can be used, but general wine merchants can provide equally appealing— and perhaps better—wine that is natural, pure and without additives. Aside from these canonical requirements, each community should evaluate these characteristics of wine:

- *type of grape*—some wines are labeled in a more generic way, but the varietal wines are often finer
- *color*—red fits the symbolic history better
- *body*—often the lighter-bodied reds taste better in the morning
- *sweet or dry*—most communities find a middle ground
- *price*

When a priest who is addicted to alcohol has been given permission to substitute grape juice for wine, the sacristan must exercise extra care. A certain chalice and cruet may have to be set aside quietly for this presider. The bottles of grape juice should be kept in a separate location. By following these practices, sacristans should be able to eliminate confusion or inadvertent use of wine instead of grape juice, or (vice versa). Even if a priest uses grape juice, the rest of the assembly shares from the eucharistic wine (placed on the altar in a flagon before the eucharistic prayer).

Chalices

The term "chalice" comes from the Latin *calix*, meaning "cup." Whether "chalice" or its translation is used matters little. Some have taken to calling the main vessel used during the eucharistic prayer the "chalice" and the smaller vessels used for communion distribution "cups." In some designs, the cup vessel rests on a base; the whole object or just the containment cup itself can be signified by either term. Such distinctions carry only local force. For our purposes, both words are used interchangeably.

In the beginning, Christian ritual cups may well have looked something like the cups of Jewish liturgy. Archeological remains indicate that they were made from a broad range of prized materials. As sharing became more and more restricted to clergy, the size of the cups was reduced. They also came to be seen as emblems and personal possessions of individual clerics rather than as common cups of the church. By the twentieth century, when mass production succeeded in proliferating certain standard and romantic forms, the rules for these vessels were quite rigid. Every chalice needed a base (with a cross traditionally on it to indicate the place to drink and later purify), a stem with a knob for holding it with thumb and forefinger joined (as in the Tridentine rite), and a containment vessel shaped like a cone. The latter was to be silver or gold, but with gold plating inside. The other parts could be of certain alternative metals.

Such cups still abound in contemporary sacristies and can continue to be used if they hold enough wine for the given liturgy. But the rules have been radically simplified. In addition to the general rules for vessels cited above (solid and noble materials, in shapes the local culture can appreciate), the *General Instruction of the Roman Missal* states:

> Chalices and other vessels that serve as receptacles for the blood of the Lord are to have a cup of nonabsorbent material. The base may be of any other solid and worthy material. . . . Vessels made from metal should ordinarily be gilded on the inside if the metal is one that rusts; gilding is not necessary if the metal is more precious than gold and does not rust. (#291, 294)

The instruction asserts that vessels for the eucharist will be made of "materials that are solid and that in the particular region are regarded as noble," and gives the conferences of bishops authority to decide which materials may be used (#290).

In selecting old and new chalices for use, we need as many as are necessary for the most crowded assembly of the year. We should evaluate their functionality, their nobility of form, their expressiveness of festivity and messianic fullness, and their congruence with other visible objects at the celebration.

Bottles for the Eucharistic Action

Wine and a small amount of water are placed in the one chalice during the preparation rite just before the eucharistic prayer. This simple action implies the presence of other vessels or bottles:

1. *Bottles for presenting wine.* The wine must be in a bottle or container when prepared before the celebration until it is presented to the presider and poured into the cup. Few if any examples of these containers exist from the first millennium, and there does not seem to have been a great deal of distinction made between the bottles of wine brought to the church by members and the vessels used to pour this wine into the chalices. In the Middle Ages, however, there is evidence of the existence of special bottles

for the presentation and pouring of wine. For a brief time some of these bottles were quite large; they quickly gave way to bottles that were much smaller (a result of the cup being reserved to the priest). Many confusing names were used for these bottles—*ampullae* (there were also *ampullae* of oils), "phials" or "vials," *vinaria* and *aquaria*, even the general term "vessel." By the time of the Renaissance, the term "cruet" was universally used where English was spoken. At roughly the same time, glass became the standard material for cruets because it was both the easy to clean and transparent. Transparency made it easy to tell whether the cruet contained wine or water. Stoppers also became normative.

Since Vatican II, the return of eucharistic cup-sharing by entire assemblies has resulted in the use of much larger bottles for the presentation of the wine. These sometimes look like large cruets but might also appear as carafes, decanters or flagons. All of these terms connote large, ornamental bottles, but the term "flagon" is most appropriate if the vessel has a handle, spout and cover. Decanters and carafes often appear noble when carried in procession and presented to the presider. Because they usually lack spouts, however, they tend to be less suited for pouring.

Every parish needs a variety of bottles for the presentation and pouring of wine: small cruets for weekday Masses and much larger cruets or flagons for larger assemblies. Though cruets are traditionally made of glass, especially in the smaller sizes, other materials also are acceptable provided they can be kept clean.

2. *Bottles for the altar table.* In some cases, one cup will contain sufficient wine for the communion of the assembly. If not, then the rest of the wine should be held in a worthy liturgical vessel and placed with the chalice and paten on the altar for the eucharistic prayer. The most appropriate bottles for this function are the larger cruets and flagons presented at the preparation rite. Parishes should have as many of these as are needed for the largest eucharistic assembly of the year. In keeping with tradition, these may be glass. They also can be of the same nonabsorbent material as the chalice—precious metal or ceramic. Some writers have suggested that glass is better because it allows all to see the sacramental sign. This argument, similarly framed in discussing vessels for the holy oils, needs to be balanced with an opposing view. We should not be focusing on seeing the elements; this is what gave us the medieval practices of the elevation and exposition.

Instead, we should see the elements only in their sharing at communion. Both arguments have strength. The job of the sacristan is to choose vessels that are made of the worthiest materials.

3. *Bottle for the water that will be added.* The mixture of wine with water, rooted in ancient Jewish custom, presumes a vessel of water prepared before Mass and given to the presider at the preparation rite. This was always a small amount of water. For centuries, when the wine vessels were also quite small, water was kept in matching cruets. These small containers, usually made of glass, are still serviceable for this minor action. Except at small gatherings, however, they should no longer match the scale of the wine vessel. It is best if this pouring of the water is kept quite distinct from the washing of the hands, with a separate ewer or pitcher reserved for that later action.

4. *Bottles for eucharistic reservation.* Eucharistic wine may be reserved in the tabernacle for sick members who are either allergic to wheat or unable to swallow with ease. This is an admirable practice but is seldom utilized, to the detriment of the sick. Bottles or flasks or pyxes (we have no set liturgical term yet) should be found or commissioned. They should exhibit a worthy design and have both a secure lid and a neck or opening that allows the eucharistic wine to be poured from a flagon or chalice into it. In addition, they should have cases that will permit them to be carried safely.

Other Requisites for the Wine

Two other types of functional equipment assist in the dignified use of cups and bottles: funnels and trays. Funnels are essential in pouring wine from a bottle or other contain into most cruets and some flagons. They should be large enough at the top so that liquids can be poured into them easily without spilling, and small enough at the bottom to fit into the mouth of the receiving vessel. They should be made of a material that can be easily cleaned. If a funnel also will be used for the pouring of consecrated wine into flasks for reservation, then its dignified appearance is important. Especially in this latter case, but in normal use as well, there might be some sort of saucer or dish on which to place the funnel.

Parishes also should have a variety of dignified-looking trays. In the past, small trays or casters, often of glass, were used to hold small cruets. They still may be used this way for smaller gatherings, but they should not be used for the washing of hands. Some communities have begun using larger trays for carrying the communion cups from the sacristy to the credence table. If the consecrated wine is poured into these cups at the altar table, the same trays might bear them from credence to altar. They should be of a noble or formal design and not resemble the trays used in self-serve restaurants.

BREAD AND VESSELS FOR BREAD

The Restoration of Communion

For many centuries, the priest was the only one eating the eucharistic banquet at many Masses, and he was mandated to do so. Other Catholics waited for special feasts, for a Sunday made special by their group's sharing in communion before a "communion breakfast," or for the obligatory reception at Eastertide. Meanwhile, they engaged in "spiritual communion," which included acts of mental prayer at the consecration, participation in eucharistic benediction, and occasional private visits to the blessed sacrament for prayer before the tabernacle.

Though there were admirable aspects to such eucharistic devotions, they eventually became more important than the sacraments themselves, than liturgical actions in general. Spiritual communion and worship of the eucharist outside of Mass were put back into perspective by the many reforms of the entire twentieth century. Pius X lowered the age for first communion. Both he and later popes pressed all Catholics to share in eucharistic communion more often. Some parishes were affected by these pleas and by the liturgical movement, and certainly no one could miss the dramatic changes in all of the church's liturgical rites in the 1960s. The return to active participation was most pronounced at the Sunday celebrations of the eucharist.

Bread

While the bread for eucharist may well have been leavened for much of the first millennium, churches of the Roman rite have been using unleavened bread for many centuries. We in the Roman rite have long been accustomed to round breads, called hosts, and to the frequent imposition of monograms or designs on the shape of these hosts. Current norms are found in the *General Instruction of the Roman Missal*:

It is most desirable that the faithful receive the Lord's body from hosts consecrated at the same Mass and that, in the instances when it is permitted, they share in the chalice. Then even through the signs communion will stand out more clearly as a sharing in the sacrifice actually being celebrated. (#56h)

The bread must be made only from wheat, and must have been baked recently; according to the long-standing tradition of the Latin church, it must be unleavened. (#282)

The nature of the sign demands that the material for the eucharistic celebration truly have the appearance of food. Accordingly, even though unleavened and baked in the traditional shape, the eucharistic bread should be made in such a way that in a Mass with a congregation the priest is able actually to break the host into parts and distribute them to at least some of the faithful. (When, however, the number of communicants is large or other pastoral needs require it, small hosts are in no way ruled out.) The action of the breaking of the bread, the simple term for the eucharist in apostolic times, will more clearly bring out the force and meaning of the sign of the unity of all in the one bread and of their charity, since the one bread is being distributed among the members of the one family. (#283)

Care must be taken to ensure that the elements are kept in good condition: that . . . the bread (does not) spoil or become too hard to be broken easily. (#285)

The major change for bread-making is in article 283. Breads should be of a much larger size so that all may share from the same loaf or host. These reforms are imbued with an appreciation of sacramental signs, and as that same appreciation permeated local churches, many communities began baking their own bread for the eucharist. There are, of course, any number of ways to moisten wheaten flour, to knead it and to bake it. (Vatican officials strongly criticized those who added ingredients other than wheat flour and water to the bread in order to make it look, taste or smell better.)

Communities that bake their own eucharistic bread might use this recipe from Dennis Krouse:

1. For 70 communicants, use ⅓ cup whole wheat flour to ⅔ cup unbleached white flour. The mixture of flour should be kept in an airtight container in the freezer and used while cold. (The cold flour helps prevent a separate crust from forming.)

2. Use one cup of the flour mixture to approximately ½ cup of naturally effervescent water (Perrier, for example). The water should be refrigerator cold.

3. Quickly mix the flour and water together with a fork until all the flour is moist. Form dough into a smooth ball. Usually more flour needs to be sprinkled on the surface of the dough to prevent stickiness.

4. Gently flatten the ball of dough into a circular loaf about ½- to ¾-inch thick. If necessary, turn any uneven edges underneath.

5. Place unscored loaf on a lightly oiled baking sheet. (Use nonstick spray and wipe off excess.)

6. Place loaf in a preheated oven at 425 degrees.

7. After approximately 12 to 15 minutes the top crust should have raised slightly. Prick the crust with a toothpick in several places, turn the loaf over and continue to bake about five minutes. (This gives an evenness to the top of the loaf.)

8. Turn the loaf right side up again and continue to bake until the crust is very lightly browned, about 10 to 15 minutes more for a total of 25 to 30 minutes. Baking time when using more than 1½ cups of flour needs to be extended.

9. Place the loaf on a rack for cooling. (You may want to slice the bottom crust off to check for undercooked dough.)

10. Bread is best when made fresh the day of the liturgy. However, after baking, it can be tightly wrapped and frozen for later use.

In parishes where a regular system of baking bread has not been implemented, hosts of various sizes are available from many commercial suppliers and religious communities. Such communities, who sometimes make this bread as their only means of support or to support their social ministries, deserve the patronage of parishes that do not bake their own bread.

No matter where the bread comes from, the sacristan must make sure that is delivered regularly and on time, and that it is baked in the largest loaves possible. Bread or hosts should be stored in canisters or other containers. Some parishes still have containers from previous decades, including those curious cylindrical ones with interior weights to keep the hosts flat. Large loaves of bread obviously will require other means of storage.

Patens or Plates for the Eucharistic Action

In the first millennium, the eucharist was distributed from the same paten or plate that contained the elements on the altar table. These were quite large and circular, holding leavened bread for the entire assembly. With the introduction of wafer-breads, these patens could be much smaller. When the communion of the faithful declined so radically in the Middle Ages, the single paten often held only the one host for the priest. As the paten became smaller, it came to be made of the same material as the chalice and in proportion to it. From this flowed the practice of placing the paten on top of the chalice before and after the eucharist, a practice that continued until the recent liturgical reforms were enacted.

As with other liturgical artifacts, the norms for patens are quite simple. In addition to the general norms for all vessels (solid and noble materials, in shapes appreciated by the local culture), the *General Instruction of the Roman Missal* notes that

> [v]essels that serve as receptacles for the eucharistic bread, such as paten, ciborium, pyx, monstrance, etc., may be made of other materials that are prized in the region, for example, ebony or other hard woods, as long as they are suited to sacred use.
>
> For the consecration of hosts one rather large paten may properly be used; on it is placed the bread for the priest as well as for the ministers and the faithful. (#292–93)

The large paten the instruction speaks of can take one of many different shapes—for example, concave plates, shallow bowls or larger vessels shaped like pie plates (but of finer materials). As is the case with one cup and any complementary flagons, additional patens are brought from the credence table during the breaking of the bread. They are filled with pieces as the loaves are broken. These patens may or may not form a matched set with the various chalices. The eucharistic bread should not be contained in anything that resembles a cup, a box or a large bowl. The terms "plate" and "paten" can be used interchangeably, but the latter is a bit more specific for eucharistic functions, although the use of this term should in no way indicate a return to the days of tiny disks of metal perched on chalice tops.

Vessels for Eucharistic Reservation

The term "pyx" can signify any one of the many containers that hold eucharistic bread for reservation. They keep the eucharistic banquet fresh and available for the absent, the sick and the dying. In the early centuries, many Christians used these vessels to bring the eucharist to their homes. In the Middle Ages, before tabernacles were regularly installed in sanctuaries, the pyx was often shaped as a dove or veiled with beautiful fabric and then suspended near the altar. On occasion, pyxes were made with base and stem.

In the fourteenth century the term "ciborium" came to be used for one variant of the pyx. Earlier this term had been used to describe the architectural canopy or roof above the altar. These new ciboria differed from many other pyxes in that their covers were loose rather than attached by hinges. They also came to resemble chalices. Like all pyxes, the purpose of the ciborium was to reserve the eucharistic bread for the sick and the dying.

In later centuries, and especially as communities began receiving communion again regularly in the twentieth century, ciboria began to be used for the consecration and distribution of communion. This modern invention was quite regrettable. Ciboria have little sign value related to bread—they look like drinking cups, not bread plates. "Stackable" ciboria also are inappropriate. They seem to have been designed to take up the least amount of room in the tabernacle rather than as artistic creations to enhance and dignify the sharing.

Each parish should own as many pyxes as are needed by the communion ministers visiting the sick. They should generally be of a smaller size, owing to the fact that long itineraries of "communion calls" rarely exist outside hospitals. The tabernacle should house whatever portions of eucharistic bread are needed for the sick, and the bread should be placed in one or more of these pyxes. Parishes should use ciboria only when the number of hosts reserved for the sick is quite large and ciboria are the largest forms of pyx available.

The distribution of eucharistic bread at Mass should be performed with the necessary number of patens, not with ciboria. As the *General Instruction* itself notes, all of the consecrated bread should be on the one paten.

Vessels for Eucharistic Exposition

In the twelfth century (and earlier), the eucharist was carried from church buildings in pyxes. Over the next few centuries, as popular devotion excited the desire of the people to see the consecrated host, formal processions and enthronements of hosts in pyxes became common. To accommodate the desire for visibility, some new pyxes included glass windows, sometimes with interior devices to prop up a host and sometimes with elaborate architectural forms.

By the fifteenth century, artistic and devotional evolution led to a new kind of pyx in which hosts were no longer propped up by some device within the windowed pyx. The new pyx was shrunk to the size of one large host and was totally transparent. Called a lunette, this pyx looked and worked something like a watch case. When not in use, the pyx could be stored in a fitted metal case called the *custodia*. When utilized for exposition, the lunette could be fitted into any one of a number of large showcases or stands called monstrances or *ostensoria*. These were often designed in the shape of the sun, with rays extending out on all sides, but other forms were used as well.

The same system of lunette-pyx, *custodia* case and monstrance-holder prevails today, but the popularity of exposition has rightly been diminished as full participation in the eucharistic action has increased. On those occasions when lunettes, *custodia* and monstrances are used, the sacristan needs to be sure that the lunette fits into the given monstrance, that the host fits into the lunette, and that the host is put out before Mass for consecration.

VESSELS FOR LITURGICAL WASHINGS

The orders for Christian liturgies were first developed and shared between communities in which ceremonial washings were common. Many civic, religious and domestic settings called for fountains or basins of water. The scriptures and the annals of early churches contain many stories of ceremonial washings of the whole body, the head, hair, the feet, and hands or fingers. Such ceremonial washings were often done after cures.

Feet

Stories of the Last Supper and traditions that called for footwashing (on Holy Thursday and at other ritual moments) have provided our current ritual with its only ceremony of washing feet—at the Evening Mass of the Lord's Supper on Holy Thursday. This action requires several towels, at least one large pitcher of warm water and at least one large basin dish. These vessels should be quite a bit larger than those used for washing hands. And even though they are used only once a year, they should be made of materials that are both serviceable and worthy.

Hands

The order of Mass still includes the minor but longstanding tradition of washing the presider's hands before the eucharistic prayer. The first word of the psalm verses (Psalm 26:6ff) formerly said during this action, *lavabo* ("I wash"), is still frequently used to describe both the action itself and the equipment used in it. Through the centuries, this washing was considered both a practical and a symbolic act.

Before Vatican II's reforms, pitchers and basins for this action were often reserved to special and episcopal liturgies (where they were often called "ewer" and "bacile"). At other Masses, the water cruet and even the cruet dish were used not only for their traditional purpose but for washing, too. The current liturgical books clearly define two containers that are used for different purposes. One is the cruet that is used in conjunction with the chalice; the other is the container of water used for the washing of hands. All parishes should have pitchers and basins (of metal, glass or other dignified material) that are used only for the washing of hands, which should not resemble the vessels that are used for the wine and water meant for drinking.

In deciding the size and number of vessels needed for the washing of hands, one should consider all of the occasions on which it is done. In some cases, several persons may need to wash their hands at more or less the same time. The most frequent handwashing is the presider's at the preparation rite of the liturgy of the eucharist. This may seem like a totally symbolic rather than practical moment, but it is in fact both. Symbolic purification and the cleansing of hands after handling various gifts presented by the community are both part of our heritage. All of the other handwashings in the current rites are more obviously practical. For some washings, the traditional addition of lemon wedges or small bars of soap is helpful. These may rest in the basin itself, or perhaps in a side dish. In general, it is better if ministers stay within the ritual areas (generally at the credence table where the equipment rests) and perform these washings with the assistance of other ministers. This is usually more dignified than disappearing into the sacristy to wash.

Handwashing supplies are usually most needed

- for the one who washes feet on Holy Thursday, right after that action (possibly with a small bar of soap);

- for the various ministers who impose ashes, right after that act (with small bars of soap); several vessels can help;

- for those performing anointings with oil (as at communal anointings of the sick, confirmation, rites of the catechumenate), if the oil is not absorbed, while the music accompanying the anointings continues and before the rest of the liturgy. (Lemon wedges are traditionally helpful here. If several ministers are performing the anointings, several basins and pitchers would be helpful. A very important principle is that the one being anointed should not have the oil wiped away after the anointing.);

- for newly-ordained priests, who may wash their hands after being anointed. This is an exception to the general rule just noted—the newly ordained cannot handle the eucharistic elements well with oily hands.

Fingers

Before the reforms, a covered "ablution cup" containing water rested beside the tabernacle. Those who had distributed the eucharist dipped their thumbs and forefingers in it after placing the ciboria in the tabernacle. These ablution cups are no longer needed for two reasons: first, sufficient bread and wine should be consecrated for each and every Mass, so there should be little traffic to the tabernacle; and second, if crumbs or drops of eucharistic elements remain on ministers' fingers, they can be brushed off into the vessels before purification or ministers can wash their hands (thumbs and forefingers are no longer specified as the only two fingers for handling the eucharist). For this, a basin and pitcher might be more dignified than a finger bowl.

Floor

Older Catholics, and especially former servers, can remember the elaborate measures that were taken if pieces of the eucharistic bread fell on the floor. The *General Instruction* simplifies matters considerably: "If the eucharistic bread or any particle of it should fall, it is to be picked up reverently. If any

of the precious blood spills, the area should be washed and the water poured into the sacrarium" (#239). The water can come from the basin at the credence table, and the cloths used with it can be extra purificators from the sacristy. This is a simple matter of wiping up the spillage, and no blame, alarm or drama should be conveyed by sacristans and ministers of communion.

OTHER VESSELS

This chapter has focused on eucharistic vessels. There are many other containers or receptacles used for rites and feasts. In any case, they are to be both worthy (beautiful in design and materials) and suited to their particular purpose in the liturgical action. Plates for the rings at marriage should express the importance of this jewelry and the festivity of the rite, but they should be made in such a way that the rings won't slip off easily. Bowls for ashes on Ash Wednesday should be deep enough to contain the ashes securely, but not so deep and narrow as to complicate the repeated insertion of the minister's fingers. Stands for the reverent display of saints' relics (reliquaries) should be large enough and attractive enough to perform that function efficiently and nobly, but neither relics nor stands should compete for attention with the main liturgical vessels. They should be positioned away from the altar and ambo, then securely stored away after the period of veneration ends.

CARE AND STORAGE OF VESSELS

Not many general rules can be set for such a wide variety of vessels. Each community should establish its own procedures for the regular care of its objects, depending on what kinds of vessels it uses. One general rule is that metal vessels should not be cleaned with paper towels or steel wool pads; they scratch the surface of the metal. Commercially produced polishes and chemicals also may do damage to metal or clay vessels. Periodically, vessels may need to be regilded or professionally polished.

Each community will also decide on the best way to store all of these vessels. A metal safe is traditionally useful for the most treasured ones. In any event, every sacristy needs cabinets with flexible shelving and countertops for preparation. A review of the contents of these cabinets should give an idea of their size to those planning to furnish a new or renovated sacristy, including the current store of bread and wine, enough cups for the largest eucharistic event (and at least one quite large cup), cruets and flagons for wine, cruets for water, funnel and saucer, trays (especially for multiple cups), pyxes for consecrated wine and for consecrated bread (some of these might be ciboria, other might be lunettes), enough patens for all communion stations, a monstrance, basins and pitchers for water, any reliquaries, and occasional dishes for symbols like rings and ashes.

4

Called to Create

CALLED BY NAME, FILLED WITH SKILL

Then Moses said to the Israelites: See, the LORD has called by name Bezalel son of Uri son of Hur, of the tribe of Judah; he has filled him with divine spirit, with skill, intelligence, and knowledge in every kind of craft, to devise artistic designs, to work in gold, silver, and bronze.

And he has inspired him to teach, both him and Oholiab son of Ahisamach, of the tribe of Dan. He has filled them with skill to do every kind of work done by an artisan or by a designer.

Bezalel and Oholiab and every skillful one to whom the LORD has given skill and understanding to know how to do any work in the construction of the sanctuary shall work in accordance with all that the LORD has commanded.

Moses then called Bezalel and Oholiab and every skillful one to whom the LORD had given skill, everyone whose heart was stirred to come to do the work; and they received from Moses all the freewill offerings that the Israelites had brought for doing the work on the sanctuary.

Exodus 35:30–32, 34–35a; 36:1–3a

MAKE PLATES AND DISHES

The LORD said to Moses: "You shall make plates and dishes for incense, and flagons and bowls with which to pour drink offerings; you shall make them of pure gold. And you shall set the bread of the Presence on the table before me always."

Exodus 25:29–30

YOU ARE HOLY, THE VESSELS ARE HOLY

I set apart twelve of the leading priests: Sherebiah, Hashabiah, and ten of their kin with them. And I weighed out to them the silver and the gold and the vessels, the offering for the house of our God that the king, his counselors, his lords, and all Israel there present had offered; I weighed out into their hand six hundred fifty talents of silver, and one hundred silver vessels and one hundred talents of gold, twenty gold bowls worth a thousand darics, and two vessels of fine polished bronze as precious as gold. And I said to them, "You are holy to the LORD, and the vessels are holy; and the silver and the gold are a freewill offering to the LORD, the God of your ancestors. Guard them and keep them until you weigh them before the chief priests and the Levites and the heads of families in Israel at Jerusalem, within the chambers of the house of the LORD." So the priests and Levites took over the silver, the gold, and the vessels as they were weighed out, to bring them to Jerusalem, to the house of our God.

Ezra 8:24–30

GOD CANNOT BE CONTAINED

Faith involves a good tension between human modes of expressive communications and God himself, whom our human tools can never adequately grasp. God transcends. God is mystery. God cannot be contained in or confined by any of our words or images or categories.

While our words and art forms cannot contain or confine God, they can, like the world itself, be icons, avenues of approach, numinous presences, ways of touching without totally grasping or seizing. Flood, fire, the rock, the sea, the mountain, the cloud, the political situations and institutions of succeeding periods—in all of them Israel touched the face of God, found help for discerning a way, moved toward the reign of justice and peace. Biblical faith assures us that God covenants a people through human events and calls the covenanted people to shape human events.

And then in Jesus, the Word of God is flesh: "This is what we proclaim to you: what was from the beginning, what we have heard, what we have seen with our eyes, what we have looked upon and our hands have touched—we speak of the word of life" (1 John 1).

Christians have not hesitated to use every human art in their celebration of the saving work of God in Jesus Christ, although in every historical period they have been influenced, at times inhibited, by cultural circumstances. In the resurrection of the Lord, all things are made new. Wholeness and healthiness are restored, because the reign of sin and death is conquered. Human limits are still real and we must be conscious of them. But we must also praise God and give God thanks with the human means we have available. God does not need liturgy; people do, and people have only their own arts and styles of expression with which to celebrate.

Environment and Art in Catholic Worship (U.S. National Conference of Catholic Bishops, Bishops' Committee on the Liturgy, 1978), 1–4

ALWAYS DESIGNED BY AN ARTIST

Sacred vessels are necessary for the celebration of the liturgy. Among these, the chalice and paten are particularly important because of the function they serve.

Sacred vessels should be fashioned from durable materials. If a metal which oxidizes (i.e. copper) is used, it should be gilded on the interior surface. Gilding is not otherwise required, unless by the nature of the design.

Vessels may be made of any valuable and appropriate material, but chalices must have a cup of nonabsorbent material.

There is no restriction, other than those of functional requirements, on the shape or decoration of sacred vessels, but because of their particular importance they should always be designed by an artist.

The Place of Worship: Pastoral Directory on the Building and Reordering of Churches (Irish Episcopal Commission for Liturgy, 1966, 1994), 21.1–21.4

THROUGH THE SPIRIT

Through the spirit of wisdom you know that created things proceed from God and that without him nothing is. Through the spirit of understanding, you have received the capacity for practical knowledge of the order, the variety, and the measure that you apply to your various kinds of work. Through the spirit of council you do not hide away the talent given to you by God, but, working and teaching openly and with humility, you faithfully reveal it to those who desire to learn. Through the spirit of fortitude you shake off all the apathy of sloth, and whatever you commence with quick enthusiasm you carry through to completion with full vigor. Through the spirit of knowledge that is given to you, you are the master by virtue of your practical knowledge and you use in public the perfect abundance of your abounding heart with the confidence of a full mind. Through the spirit of piety you set a limit with pious consideration on what the work is to be, and for whom, as well as on the time, the amount, and the quality of work, and, lest the vice of greed or cupidity should steal in, on the amount of recompense. Through the spirit of the fear of the Lord you bear in mind that of yourself you are nothing able and you ponder on the fact that you possess and desire nothing that is not given to you by God, but in faith, trust, and thankfulness you ascribe to divine compassion whatever you now are or can be.

Theophilus, metalsmith and monk (c. 1100)

MY CUP OVERFLOWS

You prepare a table before me

in the presence of my enemies;

you anoint my head with oil;

my cup overflows.

Psalm 23:5

IN CLAY VESSELS

We do not proclaim ourselves; we proclaim Jesus Christ as Lord and ourselves as your slaves for Jesus' sake. For it is the God who says, "Let light shine out of darkness," who has shown in our hearts to give the light of the knowledge of the glory of God in the face of Jesus Christ.

But we have this treasure in clay jars, so that it may be made clear that this extraordinary power belongs to God and does not come from us. We are afflicted in every way, but not crushed; perplexed, but not driven to despair; persecuted, but not forsaken; struck down, but not destroyed; always carrying in the body the death of Jesus, so that the life of Jesus may also be made visible in our bodies.

2 Corinthians 4:5–10

5

The Vessels of Margaret Fischer

ARTIST'S STATEMENT

To paraphrase Winston Churchill, I form sacred vessels and they form me. The process of creating liturgical commissions always calls me to consider my understandings of church, liturgy and community, of humanity and divinity, of spiritual and material. Each process for a commission has its own personality. Each has shown me the nobility of the human spirit and the wisdom of the collaborative process. Each has fostered in me the desire to bring the best to a worshiping community. Each shows me how the humble materials of metal and enamel can reveal the glory of God, not only in the objects themselves but also in those involved in bringing them into being.

Container for holy oil, sterling silver and tourmaline, 6" h. x 4" dia.

Reverend Robert Marrone, pastor, St. Peter Church, Cleveland, Ohio, 1991. The medieval shape complements the Gothic style of the church building.

Vessels are metaphors for Christ, the church and each of its members. Each contains its gifts to be given for the benefit of all. As Saint Paul says, "There are many gifts . . ." So each vessel must be uniquely crafted to honor those gifts and those who are to receive them. Creating the shapes, selecting the colors and materials, and choosing the techniques for fabrication all work to serve this honor. Vessels can emphasize important ritual moments for a worshiping community; well-conceived vessels that are made for that community bring it to a deeper appreciation and experience of God's love poured out for his people.

John Buscemi set the tone for my approach to working on liturgical vessels and, indeed, to all my artwork and other endeavors as well. I heard him talk about "artist as servant" in a presentation once. Whatever effort one undertakes, if it seeks to serve God, its benefactors, and the purpose for which it is created, it is rightly conceived. If lesser concerns take over, the work will be compromised and fail to fulfill its function properly.

Vessel for the oil of the sick, sterling, 2½" dia. x 2" h.

Reverend David Novak, pastor, Holy Trinity Church, Lorain, Ohio, 1990. The design on the cover alludes to dripping oil.

(Right, and on facing page) Tabernacle, cloisonné enamel, 14" h. x 10" dia.

Magnificat Chapel, Sisters of the Humility of Mary, Villa Maria, Pennsylvania, 1995. The source of the design is Psalm 141: "Let my prayer rise like incense."

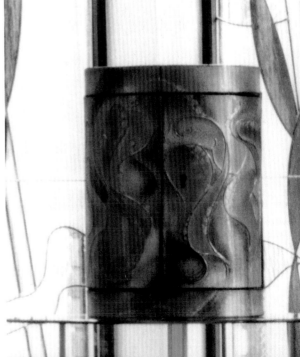

Representative pieces from a communion set, enamel on copper. Large cup, 6½" h. x 7½" dia.; large paten, 2" deep x 9½" dia.; small cup, 6" h. x 4" dia.; small paten, 1" deep x 8" dia.

Church of the Resurrection, Salon, Ohio, 1984. The complete set includes one large cup and paten (both pictured), six small patens and eight small cups. The number of pieces allows for an easy flow during the communion rite. The ample size of the large pieces reflects the concept "one bread, one cup." The colors work with the muted earth tones of the church building.

Paten, enamel on copper, 1" deep x 10" dia., 1992.

The surface design alludes to the nature of the eucharist as everlasting love.

Incense burner, enamel on copper, 6" h. x 6" dia., 1978.

The open shape allows for a generous circulation of incense.

Kiddush cup, enamel on copper, 4½" h. x 3" dia.

Ohio Craft Museum, Columbus, Ohio, 1985. The cup is used at the first seder of Passover at the place set for Elijah.

(Left, and detail below) Chalice and paten, cloisonné enamel. Chalice, 6" h. x 4" dia.

This set bridges the traditional and contemporary.

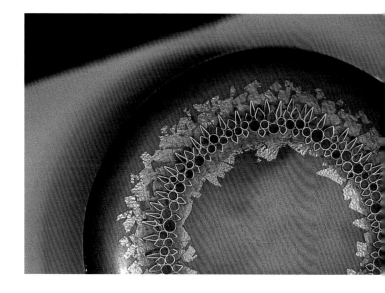

6

The Vessels of
William Frederick

ARTIST'S STATEMENT

Having come to metalworking from a background in engineering and industrial design (studying at the Massachusetts Institute of Technology and the Art Institute of Chicago, as well as in industry itself), in which the design limits are prescribed and narrow, it has been with a great sense of freedom that I have thrown myself into the design and execution of custom-designed liturgical vessels and objects. Like industry and engineering, however, the client has input in the artistic process and in its final expression. After one or more discussion as to what the object is to do and say, I produce drawings that express its purpose differently. The client makes a selection, and together we may make refinements, although I retain control of the esthetic expression.

Chalice, bronze and gold, 7" h., 1980.

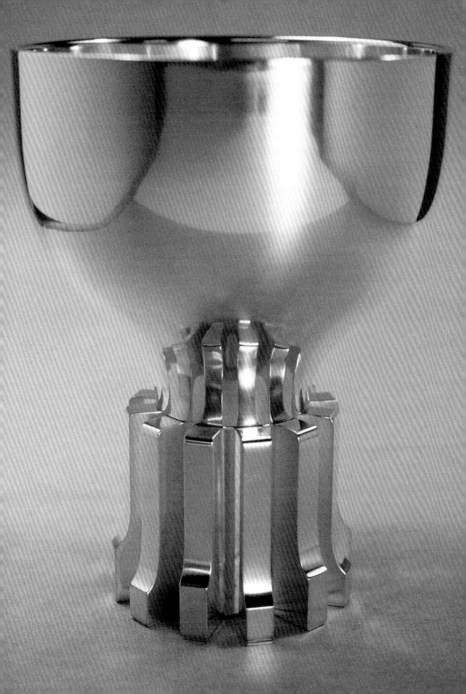

The piece is then made using only hand tools in the manner of the Arts and Crafts metalsmiths. I find the challenge of making the finished piece as close to the selected design as possible exciting, although the design process itself, in which the goal is to try to create something fresh and new, is no less exciting. I have been told that there are no new shapes, that what I'm doing is futile. I think it has to do with what one believes.

My philosophy in making objects used in the liturgy involves the human dimension — the honest expression of the characteristics of the materials involved (melted surfaces in lost wax casting, hammered surfaces on objects that are hand-formed, and so on). For example, it is not possible to hand-form a chalice cup without leaving work marks in the surface at the end. To make it smooth for drinking, it has to be hammered (planished). Each metalsmith will produce a different visual result in this process, making it personal. It is, in effect, a signature: honest, human, contemporary and Christian. Hammered surfaces can be filed smooth and polished in imitation of machine-made objects, but the end result is, in a sense, dishonest to the craft and the artist.

Pyx, sterling with appliqué, 2½" dia.

Reverend E. Sedliecki, 1977.

Chalice, hand-hammered silver base, 6" h.

Private collection.

Tabernacle, gold-plated sterling, 12" x 12" x 22" h.

SS. Peter and Paul Greek Orthodox Church, Glenview, Illinois, 1984.

Chalice, bright-cut appliqué, gold-plated sterling silver, amethysts, 7 ½" h.

Reverend Ed Moszur, 1996.

(Facing page) Funerary urn, bronze and applied sterling, 12" h. x 8" across.

Morton Knopf, Chicago, 1999.

Chalice, sterling cup, cast-bronze cradle, 6½" h.

St. Vincent Ferrer Church, New York, 1973.

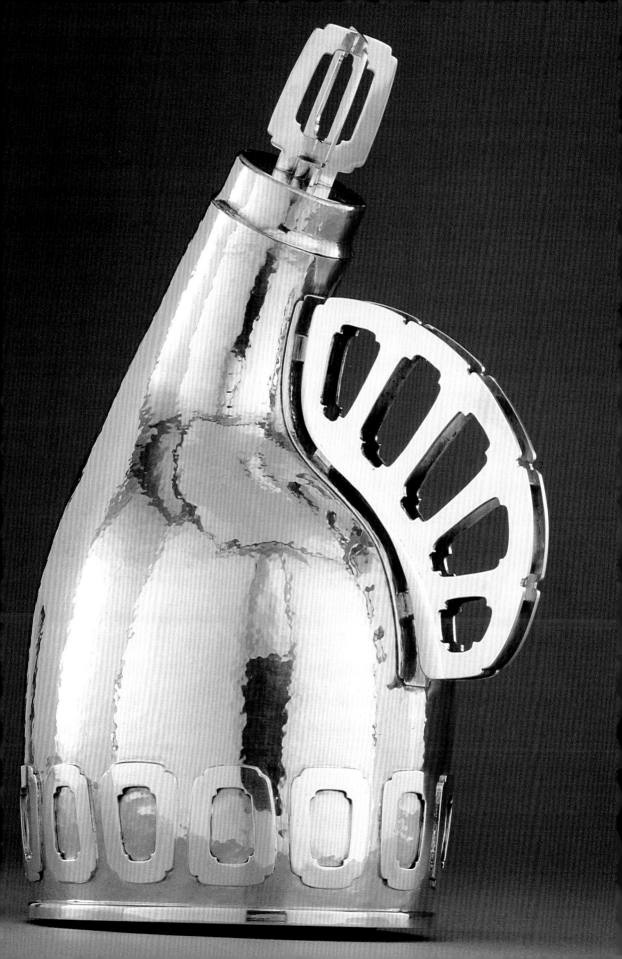

7

The Vessels of
Mark Humenick

ARTIST'S STATEMENT

I try to make my work a prayer. I ask for the intercession of Saint Dunstan, my patron saint, on each project. The finished piece is merely a translation of the needs of the church patron, and it should communicate on three levels: esthetic, technical and functional. Each piece is approached individually because each need is unique. While some artists find technical and functional considerations too limiting, I welcome the challenge. A vessel *must* work; I could work a lifetime on just one chalice and never come to a perfect solution.

My materials are natural and traditional, such as silver, copper and gemstones. Metal is a slow medium, and its manipulation gives time for meditation. Precious metals and gems are among the most ancient and recycled gifts from God; how they are employed makes the artistic statement. The role of the artist is to define the esthetic of tomorrow.

Jubilee Chalice; **fabricated and raised
sterling silver, garnet, amethyst and citrine;
12" h. x 5" dia., 1998.**

A metal vessel is an object that reflects light. If a single person comes closer to God by seeing a shimmer of light when the chalice is elevated, then my work is complete.

I view technique as a huge cabinet with many drawers. To accomplish an idea, I go to a particular drawer for the solution. Experience adds more drawers. Different techniques cannot provide the main focus of the piece, however; they are only tools.

"Metal is my vocabulary.
Technique is my grammar.
The work is my psalm."

Abbey Set; fabricated and raised sterling silver, vermeil and garnets; chalice, 5¼" dia. x 5¾" h.

Commissioned by Archbishop Michael J. Sheehan for the raising to an abbey of Christ in the Desert, Abiquiu, New Mexico, 1996.

Canticle of Saint Francis Set; raised and cast sterling silver, moonstone, black sapphire, citrine, turquoise, garnet, tourmaline and iolite; chalice, 7" h. x 4½" dia.

Reverend Manuel Viera, 1998.

Mother of God Set; raised and cast sterling silver and azure blue star sapphires; chalice, 6½" h. x 4" dia.

Reverend Jeffery Haltman, Siegel, Illinois, 1995.

Friar's Chalice Set; fabricated, raised and cast sterling silver and turquoise inlay; chalice, 6" h. x 4" dia.

Commissioned for the 75th anniversary of the Franciscan friars' return to St. Francis Cathedral, Santa Fe, New Mexico, 1995.

Incense bowl; copper, brass and malachite; 12" h. x 10 w.; 1996.

Oil flagon, reverse raised copper and recycled copper engraving plates, 7" h. x 4" w., 1979.

Incense bowl; hot forged and machined copper, brass and lapis lazuli; 16" h. x 7" w.; 1996.

(Facing page) *Monastery Monstrance;* fabricated and machined brass, gold plate, garnet and amethyst; 34" h. x 16" w.

8

The Vessels of Marirose Jelicich

ARTIST'S STATEMENT

I have always been interested in three-dimensional sculptural forms. I like the cleanness of black and white, and the purity of form that I define as uncluttered, exquisitely beautiful and simple yet functional.

As an artist, I experimented with different materials until I found one that I was both comfortable with and challenged by: metals, especially sterling silver. My two favorite parts of the process are the casting and fabricating stages. Working with the two processes together or singly gives one almost unlimited design possibilities, keeping in mind that a piece requires both good design and craftsmanship. If either is lacking the piece will not be successful. Client satisfaction is also important, stimulating creativity in the execution of the piece.

Easter fire brazier, Cor-Ten steel, 5' x 7'.

St. Paschal Baylon, Oakland, California, 1994.

I believe vessels should enhance and raise one's esthetic awareness in the Christian community. With care, the liturgy's vessels will last a lifetime, and even pass on to the next generation the beauty and simplicity of functional art forms that are pregnant with the memories of those who made them possible.

(Facing page) Monstrance with 9" lunette, sterling silver and brass.

St. Philip the Apostle, Bakersfield, California, 1993.

Holy Thursday foot-washing bowl and pitcher, powdercoated aluminum.

San Carlos Cathedral, Monterey, California, 1998.

Glass holy oils vessels with semi-precious stones.

San Carlos Cathedral, Monterey, California, 1998.

Communion set; glass, sterling silver and black Virginia soapstone.

Bishop D. Ryan, Monterey, California, 1994.

Communion set, brass with semi-precious stones.

St. Catherine of Siena, Vallejo, California, 1993.

9

Attention and Care

COVER AND CARRY

The LORD spoke to Moses and Aaron, saying: "When the camp is to set out, Aaron and his sons shall go in and take down the screening curtain, and cover the ark of the covenant with it; then they shall put on it a covering of fine leather, and spread over that a cloth all of blue, and shall put its poles in place. Over the table of the bread of the Presence they shall spread a blue cloth, and put on it the plates, the dishes for incense, the bowls, and the flagons for the drink offering; the regular bread also shall be on it; then they shall spread over them a crimson cloth, and cover it with a covering of fine leather, and shall put its poles in place. They shall take a blue cloth, and cover the lampstand for the light, with its lamps, its snuffers, its trays, and all the vessels for oil with which it is supplied; and they shall put it with all its utensils in a covering of fine leather, and put it on the carrying frame.

"When Aaron and his sons have finished covering the sanctuary and all the furnishings of the sanctuary, as the camp sets out, after that the Kohathites shall come to carry these, but they must not touch the holy things, or they will die."

Numbers 4:1, 5–10, 15

THE VESSELS OF GOD'S TEMPLE

King Belshazzar made a great festival for a thousand of his lords, and he was drinking wine in the presence of the thousand.

Under the influence of the wine, Belshazzar commanded that they bring in the vessels of gold and silver that his father Nebuchadnezzar had taken out of the temple in Jerusalem, so that the king and his lords, his wives, and his concubines might drink from them. So they brought in the vessels of gold and silver that had been taken out of the temple, the house of God in Jerusalem, and the king and his lords, his wives, and his concubines drank from them. They drank the wine and praised the gods of gold and silver, bronze, iron, wood, and stone.

Immediately the fingers of a human hand appeared and began writing on the plaster of the wall of the royal palace, next to the lampstand. The king was watching the hand as it wrote. Then the king's face turned pale, and his thoughts terrified him. His limbs gave way, and his knees knocked together. The king cried aloud to bring in the enchanters, the Chaldeans, and the diviners; and the king said to the wise men of Babylon, "Whoever can read this writing and tell me its interpretation shall be clothed in purple, have a chain of gold around his neck, and rank third in the kingdom." Then all the king's wise men came in, but they could not read the writing or tell the king the interpretation. Then King Belshazzar became greatly terrified and his face turned pale, and his lords were perplexed.

The queen, when she heard the discussion of the king and his lords, came into the banqueting hall. The queen said, "O king, live forever! Do not let your thoughts terrify you or your face grow pale. There is a man in your kingdom who is endowed with a spirit of the holy gods. In the days of your father he was found to have enlightenment, understanding, and wisdom like the wisdom of the gods. Your father, King Nebuchadnezzar, made him chief of the magicians, enchanters, Chaldeans, and diviners, because an excellent spirit, knowledge, and understanding to interpret dreams, explain riddles, and solve problems were found in this Daniel, whom the king named Belteshazzar. Now let Daniel be called, and he will give the interpretation."

Then Daniel was brought in before the king. The king said to Daniel, "So you are Daniel, one of the exiles of Judah, whom my father the king brought from Judah? I have heard of you that a spirit of the gods is in you, and that enlightenment, understanding, and excellent wisdom are found in you. Now the wise men, the enchanters, have been brought in before me to read this writing and tell me its interpretation, but they were not able to give the interpretation of the matter. But I have heard that you can give interpretations and solve problems. Now if you are able to read the writing and tell me its interpretation, you shall be clothed in purple, have a chain of gold around your neck, and rank third in the kingdom."

Then Daniel answered in the presence of the king, "Let your gifts be for yourself, or give your rewards to someone else! Nevertheless I will read the writing to the king and let him know the interpretation. O king, the Most High God gave your father Nebuchadnezzar kingship, greatness, glory, and majesty. And because of the greatness that he gave him, all peoples, nations, and languages trembled and feared before him. He killed those he wanted to kill, kept alive those he wanted to keep alive, honored those he wanted to honor, and degraded those he wanted to degrade. But when his heart was lifted up and his spirit was hardened so that he acted proudly, he was deposed from his kingly throne, and his glory was stripped from him. He was driven from human society, and his mind was made like that of an animal. His dwelling was with the wild asses, he was fed grass like oxen, and his body was bathed with the dew of heaven, until he learned that the Most High God has sovereignty over the kingdom of mortals, and sets over it whomever he will. And you, Belshazzar his son, have not humbled your heart, even though you knew all this! You have exalted yourself against the Lord of heaven! The vessels of his temple have been brought in before you, and you and your lords, your wives and your concubines have been drinking wine from them. You have praised the gods of silver and gold, of bronze, iron, wood, and stone, which do not see or hear or know; but the God in whose power is your very breath, and to whom belong all your ways, you have not honored.

"So from his presence the hand was sent and this writing was inscribed. And this is the writing that was inscribed: MENE, MENE, TEKEL, and PARSIN. This is the interpretation of the matter: MENE, God has numbered the days of your kingdom and brought it to an end; TEKEL, you have been weighed on the scales and found wanting; PERES, your kingdom is divided and given to the Medes and Persians."

Then Belshazzar gave the command, and Daniel was clothed in purple, a chain of gold was put around his neck, and a proclamation was made concerning him that he should rank third in the kingdom.

That very night Belshazzar, the Chaldean king, was killed. And Darius the Mede received the kingdom, being about sixty-two years old.

Daniel 5

ATTENTION AND CARE

In a eucharistic celebration, the vessels for the bread and the wine deserve attention and care. Just as in other types of celebration those objects which are central in the rite are a natural focus. When the eucharistic assembly is large, it is desirable not to have the additional plates and cups necessary for communion on the altar. A solution is to use one large breadplate and either one large chalice or a large flagon until the breaking of the bread. At the fraction, any other chalices or plates needed are brought to the altar. While the bread is broken on sufficient plates for sharing, the ministers of the cup pour from the flagon into communion chalices. The number and design of such vessels will depend on the size of the community they serve. To eat and drink is of the essence of the symbolic fullness of this sacrament. Communion under one kind is an example of the minimizing of primary symbols.

Like the plates and chalices or flagons, all other vessels and implements used in the liturgical celebration should be of such quality and design that they speak of the importance of the ritual action. Pitchers, vessels for holy oils, bowls, cruets, sprinklers, censers, baskets for collection, etc.—all are presented to the assembly in one way or another and speak well or ill of the deed in which the assembly is engaged.

Environment and Art in Catholic Worship *(U.S. National Conference of Catholic Bishops, Bishops' Committee on the Liturgy, 1978), 96–97*

QUALITY AND APPROPRIATENESS

An important part of contemporary Church renewal is the awareness of the community's recognition of the sacred. Environment and art are to foster this awareness. Because different cultural and subcultural groups in our society may have quite different styles of artistic expression, one cannot demand any universal sacred forms.

This is not to say that liturgy makes no demand upon architecture, music and the other arts. To be true to itself and to protect its own integrity, liturgy must make demands. Basically, its demands are two: *quality* and *appropriateness*.

Whatever the style or type, no art has a right to a place in liturgical celebration if it is not of high quality and if it is not appropriate (see *General Instruction of the Roman Missal*, 254).

Quality is perceived only by contemplation, by standing back from things and really trying to *see* them, trying to let them speak to the beholder. Cultural habit has conditioned the contemporary person to look at things in a more pragmatic way: "What is it worth?" "What will it do?" Contemplation sees the hand stamp of the artist, the honesty and care that went into an object's making, the pleasing form and color and texture. Quality means love and care in the making of something, honesty and genuineness with any materials used, and the artist's special gift in producing a harmonious whole, a well-crafted work. This applies to music, architecture, sculpture, painting, pottery making, furniture making, as well as to dance, mime or drama—in other words, to any art form that might be employed in the liturgical environment or action.

Appropriateness is another demand that liturgy rightfully makes upon any art that would serve its action. The work of art must be appropriate in two ways: (1) it must be capable of bearing the weight of mystery, awe, reverence, and wonder which the liturgical action expresses; (2) it must clearly *serve* (and not interrupt) ritual action, which has its own structure, rhythm and movement.

The first point rules out anything trivial and self-centered, anything fake, cheap or shoddy, anything pretentious or superficial. That kind of appropriateness, obviously, is related to quality. But it demands more than quality. It demands a kind of transparency, so that we see and experience both the work of art and something beyond it.

Environment and Art in Catholic Worship *(U.S. National Conference of Catholic Bishops, Bishops' Committee on the Liturgy, 1978), 18–22*

CLEAN THE INSIDE OF THE CUP

Jesus said, "Woe to you, scribes and Pharisees, hypocrites! For you clean the outside of the cup and of the plate, but inside they are full of greed and self-indulgence. You blind Pharisee! First clean the inside of the cup, so that the outside also may become clean."

Matthew 23:25–26

10

Thinking about Vessels

Mark Humenick

Confusion of styles reigns in many places of worship: A replica of a twelfth-century chalice rests on a contemporary altar, and at communion time several mismatched chalices are brought forward, making the altar look like a resale counter. A Gothic monstrance with towering points find its way into a new chapel with clean lines—and looks out of place.

When a parish undertakes renovation or new construction, the furnishings and accessories are not usually thought of as part of the total environment. Often, choices are made based on personal tastes (of the pastor, committee members or patron) rather than on an understanding of the environment as a whole. Stylistic confusion implies a lack of awareness of the total environment's unity, and symbolism is impaired when styles from various eras or cultures are mixed haphazardly. Worship is an experience of unity—of communion—and so harmony of style is important in creating the proper environment for the assembly to celebrate its liturgy with beauty and grace.

St. Peter's Chalice,
**inlayed and raised
sterling silver and
river rock, 6" h. x
3½" dia.**

Methodist Community,
Florida, 1994.

EXAMPLES OF HARMONIOUS DESIGNS

Visual forms communicate at all levels. A subtle design element can communicate well beyond its literal inspiration. Consider the fluted base of a Gothic chalice: It is extremely large in proportion to the stem, node and cup. Does this signify the foundation of the building? Is its purpose to exaggerate the height of the chalice and embody the concept of reaching toward God, as Gothic architecture does? Or is the size of the base merely functional, designed so that the voluminous folds of Gothic chasubles would not accidentally tip over the chalice? Maybe all the above—and more—were the intentions of the original design, or even the design's unintended, yet no less real, results.

Take as another example a basic pillar form, such as that incorporated into the screen behind the altar at St. Francis Cathedral, Santa Fe, New Mexico. The large contemporary reredos was carved by Roberto Lavadie and frames icons of saints of the Americas painted by Robert Lentz. The pillar form creates separate panels for the paintings and also creates a good sense of scale in what is actually a large piece. Is the pillar form a Spanish-Moorish design, evoking the ethnic heritage of the first colonists? Is it an abstracted version of the rope that Franciscans wear as a cincture and that functions as a logo? Or is it both?

In 1996 I completed a new reliquary for the same cathedral's relic of Saint Francis. La Villa Real de Santa Fe de San Francisco de Asís was celebrating the centennial of the cathedral's consecration, the seventy-fifth anniversary of the return of the Franciscan friars to the parish, and the feast day of Saint Francis of Assisi. The old reliquary was a pot metal, gold-plated and mass-produced 50-year-old object that was falling apart and did not fit visually into the unusual building (a Gothic/Romanesque structure in the heart of an adobe town center). Because the main visual element of the cathedral's renovated interior is the altar screen, the reliquary needed to take its stylistic cue from that object.

First, materials had to be chosen. Silver, copper, tin (for brass), turquoise and garnets are all mined in the area of the original archdiocese. Hence, these natural materials are familiar to residents of New Mexico and also have come to represent spiritual qualities. Silver represents innocence and holiness; copper adds warmth, the hue of which mirrors the wood of the altar screen. The gold color of brass is the symbol of the divine or celestial light and glory of God, and it works with the gold-leaf background of the icons on the altar screen. The red of the garnets signifies the blood of Christ and the stigmata of Saint Francis.

Forming these elements was next. The form of the reliquary is a cross, which signifies the stigmata of Saint Francis; the placement and shape (*cabochon navette*) of the red garnets reinforce this symbolism. The number of stones (three) represents the Trinity. The rope borders of silver and copper evoke and echo the altar screen's pillar carvings. They also evoke Spanish/ Moorish design and the Franciscan community: an interpretation of the peoples, both natives and newcomers. The sun rays, along with the shell forms immediately surrounding the relic, mirror the top element of the altar screen.

The choice of materials allowed for artistic expression in finish, texture, scale, technique and detail. I find it more challenging and rewarding to work within a set of limits such as these.

A QUESTION OF MATERIALS

Why use metal to create vessels for the liturgy? Gold and silver have always been precious metals, and platinum was added to the list in the eighteenth century after it was discovered in the Americas. These metals are "precious" not only because of their monetary value but for their technical value as well.

Gold is the most ductile (able to be drawn into wire) and malleable (able to be hammered into thin sheets) of all metals. A thimbleful of gold can be drawn into a wire thinner than a human hair without breaking—and it would be a mile long! It can also be hammered or rolled so thin (0.000005 of an inch) that it becomes a translucent foil (gold leaf). Silver has the same properties and is second only to gold. It is, however, the most reflective of all metals. A "black finish," a finish that allows silver to reflect almost all the light that hits it, can be obtained by polishing. When fine silver is applied to the back of glass, it creates a mirror.

Other metals are combined with gold and silver to make alloys, which improve their durability and strength. Copper is often added to gold and silver, and when combined with tin and other metals makes the alloys brass and bronze. Brass is excellent for machining; bronze is excellent for casting. Gold and silver in their pure states do not oxidize (tarnish); the added metals do, however, as in karat gold and sterling silver. That is why gold leaf applied to an outdoor surface will last 100 years more (as on the dome at the University of Notre Dame). Pure gold and silver plating are often applied to prevent oxidation. A lacquer is applied on top of these and on other metals such as brass and bronze. These coatings wear away over time and hamper repairs or modifications. Some of the new polymer coatings for metals show greater promise for articles that are not subject to daily use.

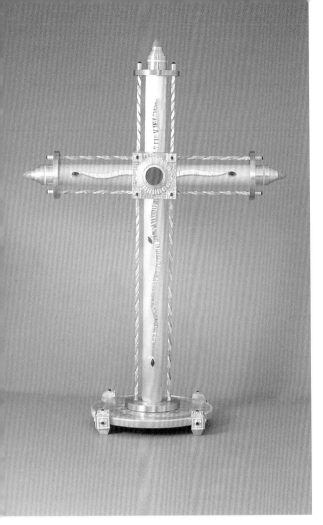

St. Francis Reliquary; **fabricated and cast sterling silver, copper, brass, turquoise and garnets; 18½" h. x 11½" w.**

St. Francis Cathedral, Santa Fe, New Mexico, 1995.

MATERIAL HANDED DOWN

Gold and silver are the most recycled gifts from God. The odds are very high that the ring you are wearing contains a portion of gold from an ancient civilization. All the refined gold in the world today would cover a baseball diamond with about three feet of gold. Conversely, we throw metals away every day in the form of labels on cosmetics, greeting cards and photographic film.

The Christian community has an obligation to praise the glory of God with all its gifts, including the vessels and objects used in its celebrations and rituals. The process of creating or finding these vessels and objects should be carried out in concert with the people and should not be elitist. A simple explanation of the need for a new object, as well as its purpose and symbolism, will greatly enhance the involvement and support of the community.

Communion vessels, gospel book covers, processional crosses and oil containers all should be designed and crafted to reflect the prayer of a particular community. Both universal and local symbolism should be incorporated into designs; this can be accomplished through form, color and the use of local materials. When the time comes, as the liturgy and the parish change, the vessels can then be modified or remade from the original metals.

DONATED METALS AND GEMS

When planning for vessels, the metals used can be supplied by the members of the parish. Has anyone looked into their dresser drawers lately and found jewelry no longer worn? How many broken chains and single earrings are there? How many sterling flatware sets are really used? Imagine the feeling a family would have knowing that the small article that they gave, a symbol of human love, is now a physical part of the celebration of God's love.

Information is essential to a successful recycling of jewelry into liturgical vessels. How the gathered jewelry will be used must be explained. Furthermore, a simple system for gathering, testing and valuing these items can provide the resources for the new designs. Gold- and silversmiths return quantities of filings, polishing dust and small unused scraps to their refiners and exchange it for newly refined (purified) metal. The typical return from a refinery is 97 percent pure metal value. The refining charge drops as the quantity increases. New portable electronic scales and metal testers can give a fairly accurate account of the quantity and quality of the metal to be refined. This system can be used in a parish program, and records of the donations can be provided easily to donors.

The gemstones in donated jewelry can be verified and evaluated by a gemologist and then incorporated into the design or returned to the parishioner. They could also be sold to fund another project or works of charity.

TRUSTING THE ARTIST

When commissioning vessels for liturgy, selecting a competent metalsmith and artist is essential. The artist who designs the work should be the one who executes it. The metalsmith/artist has a serious design responsibility: The work must be a prayer to God and must communicate to people in a contemporary way, all while serving the liturgical action. A good designer/artisan is merely an interpreter. He or she should have a knowledge of the intended use, regulation and traditions (history) of the article to be produced. Local traditions and any local input should be explained to the artist. The resulting work—vessels designed for a particular community to be part of a harmonious environment—will communicate something of God and sacrament on many levels: spiritual, symbolic, technical, functional and esthetic.

11

Ambries and the Oil Stocks

Peter Mazar

Three different parishes I know of have made an effort to reserve the holy oils and sacred chrism in a reverent manner. In one, the stocks are kept in the tabernacle of an old side altar now dedicated for that purpose. In another, a niche for holding the stocks is part of the design of the new font. In a third, the oils and chrism are held in a big, beautiful, glass-enclosed ambry that sits in a spacious gathering area, connecting in one direction with the social hall and library, and in another direction with the baptistry, which leads into the eucharistic hall. And at all three of these parishes, smaller, easier-to-use ancillary vessels filled with the oils and chrism are kept in a sacristy cupboard and taken from there for anointings!

The danger in these examples is that the efforts to recover the symbol of olive oil are for nought but show. The large ambry and abundant oil stocks become little more than props for the baptistry. We should instead design ambries and oil stocks to be both usable and beautiful.

ANCILLARY VESSELS AND A SHELF

It may be necessary to fill ancillary vessels before each use and then return the oil to the larger stock afterward, in which case the empty, smaller vessels are stored in a sacristy with other sacred vessels. But why can't filled, ancillary vessels—the ones frequently used for hospital visits and emergency anointings—also be kept in the ambry? It's not inappropriate to keep oil stocks of several sizes stored reverently in an ambry.

Of course, these smaller vessels need to be beautiful, designed for their purposes, not too small yet transportable, and airtight. And they need to be kept clean: No wads of cotton lurking inside. (There is no longer any use for, nor any way to adapt, those oil-of-catechumen-and-chrism sets used at baptisms a generation ago. These should be retired.)

Also, there needs to be a "work surface" near the ambry. Decanting oil takes a steady hand, and I often need the benefit of a sink with hot water, soap and towels—a "liturgical kitchen." I liked having the old side altar (it was more like a shelf) as part of the ambry. It gave me a fine surface for doing such things as decanting oil into ancillary vessels and keeping them handy for use during liturgy. On some occasions the surface held lit candles, flowers and an appropriate icon.

ONE OR THREE?

I once saw a church with three different ambries, one each for the chrism, the oil of catechumens and the oil of the sick. That's a good idea. The three oils are put to three different purposes, so why confuse the three by storing them together? If the church complex can accommodate three suitable, reverent locations, then why not? Each spot might then include suitable iconography, such as an image of the baptism of the Lord, Pentecost or the anointing of David for the chrism; the cure of the man born blind (or other scriptures that point to spiritual healing and strengthening) for the oil of catechumens; and the Good Samaritan for the oil of the sick.

Permanent art is not the only decoration for ambries either. For example, there are suggestions for ornamenting the ambry for every season of the church year in *To Crown the Year* (Chicago: LTP, 1995). My favorite festival ornamentation is to use fresh olive branches or at least branches of other members of the olive family, such as lilac, forsythia, osmanthus, privet, eleagnus and Russian olive, all known for the intense fragrance of their flowers.

LOCATIONS

An ambry has to go somewhere, but should the ambry automatically go in the baptistry? It isn't being overly cautious to be concerned that glass jugs of oil might be dangerous near a font. (I say this because twice over the years I've had to clean up oily accidents, once on Holy Thursday and once on Holy Saturday. The Thursday accident was with chrism, which fortuitously made the building smell wonderful and started a local tradition of perfuming the place before holidays.)

There's no special appropriateness in storing the oil of the sick near the font, and there seems to be a very good reason to store the oil of catechumens away from the font: It's the oil of strength for the journey to the font. Why not reserve the oil of the catechumens in the room where the catechumens meet weekly to break open the word? Of course, this is difficult to do if that room is used for a variety of other purposes. But when they are dismissed from the assembly, the catechumens go with a catechist to continue reflecting on the word of God. Where they go should be more a chapel than a classroom. And if that chapel is dedicated to this ministry, it would be most appropriate for it to hold an ambry for this holy oil.

Of course, the chrism in the ambry (no matter where it's located) is meant to be used at baptisms and confirmations. I think we need to clearly see it being put to use: Light the ambry brightly and ornament it for the occasion, and—as a visible part of the rite—pour the chrism from the main stock into any smaller vessel. The same should be true of the other oils used in their respective rites.

RESERVE OR DISPLAY?

Ambries that function as "monstrances" for the oils may be a good idea, but the notion of a display case is troublesome. It's beautiful to see glass vessels sparkling with light. It's also wonderful to be able to see our sacred substances; there is certainly the need to build up parish awareness and piety for the church's sacramental materials, and one way to do that is to put the materials in a place where they appear to be our common property (an idea that has for a long time left me wondering about the nature of the sacristy, which perhaps should be more than a private dressing room).

However, when an ambry looks like a display case, it evokes a museum. I think of Charlemagne's sword or a Gutenberg Bible or other wonderful things that we would never think of putting to use. I also think of the monstrance, as if the oils were being exposed for continual veneration (but with no expectation that parishioners would do so).

Why is it appropriate to put chrism in a glass ambry but inappropriate (in fact, against liturgical law) to put eucharistic bread in a transparent tabernacle?

The chrism is also "consecrated" by the bishop at the Chrism Mass on Holy Thursday (or, as is usually the case, on another day during Holy Week). This different treatment reminds me that we have developed a tremendous piety for the eucharistic bread (with all sorts of rules and traditions) without similar, deeply held attitudes toward the chrism and the way it is used and stored.

TRADITIONS OLD AND EMERGENT

It's true that there once were traditions surrounding the chrism and oils. At ordinations there was the strangely lovely practice of wrapping anointed hands with linen strips that were saved and eventually (and affectionately) buried with the priest's mother. And at confirmations we had the thoroughly antisacramental practice of wiping the chrism off with cotton balls that were then burned.

Perhaps we are working on new (and more reverent) traditions as we become more familiar with the various rites that include anointing and as we grow in knowledge and affection for the imagery of the chrism and oils. The good news is that more and more parish ministers are concerned that the chrism be fresh, fragrant and used abundantly as a spiritual "robe of glory."

Putting the oils in a display-case ambry is a kind of catechetical device (it's more than that, too, of course). I'd go so far as to label the containers in English (and not use initials) because we still need much basic catechesis about the chrism and oils. These substances are too often confused even by people who should know better. This past year I heard complaints about how the diocese "put all that good-smelling stuff into the chrism but forgot to add anything to the oil of the sick." (Chrism is a mixture of oil and perfume—the "good-smelling stuff." The oil of the sick and the oil of catechumens are supposed to be plain oil.)

DIFFERENT OILS, DIFFERENT VESSELS

It is a mistake not to distinguish by way of design and materials the vessels used for the sacred chrism and those for the two oils. Having the same or even very similar vessels unintentionally implies the wrong thing about the oils (that they are all the same): It mixes apples with oranges, so to speak. Maybe in this case the expression should be "mixes perfume (or embalming fluid), medicine

and liniment." Using similar vessels for all the oils misses the opportunity to nonverbally communicate something about their unique meanings and uses.

The chrism especially is a different "species" from the two oils. We "bless" the oils, but we "consecrate" the chrism, which we call by several additional titles, such as "oil of gladness" and "oil of thanksgiving" (because a eucharistic prayer is said over it at its consecration).

Olive oil is homey stuff used in cooking and once used as fuel for lamps, as skin conditioner and as dressing for wounds. (The Good Samaritan used olive oil to salve the man mugged by thieves. You can still find tiny bottles of olive oil in drug stores in the "ear care" section.) In classical times, having a productive olive grove came to be synonymous with peaceful and productive times. No wonder the dove plucked an olive branch to herald reconciliation!

The perfume in chrism is costly. It imparts the imagery not of homeyness but of luxury and majesty, and something else as well: embalming, which drives away the stench of death. In 2 Corinthians 2:14–17, we are given what might be called a theology of the imagery of fragrance:

> Thanks be to God, who in Christ always leads us in triumphal procession, and through us spreads in every place the fragrance that comes from knowing him. For we are the aroma of Christ to God among those who are being saved and among those who are perishing; to the one a fragrance from death to death, to the other a fragrance from life to life. . . . For we are not peddlers of God's word like so many; but in Christ we speak as persons of sincerity, as persons sent from God and standing in his presence.

Chrism needs a tightly closed bottle to keep the aroma from evaporating. Olive oil needs cool conditions to keep it from getting rancid.

Why shouldn't the vessel used for the chrism remind us of expensive perfume? Or the vessel for the sick somehow look medicinal, like an apothecary crock? The vessel for the oil of catechumens might even have athletic associations—the oil is supposed to limber us up to struggle against doubt and the devil. In any case, I think the chrism's vessel should be exquisite and extravagant (which may be the qualities of a glass or crystal vessel), while the vessels for the two oils should appear much more plain—a handsome vessel of the domestic and earthy sort (which doesn't suggest glass as the material to my way of thinking).

Not only do I think the vessels should be designed to reflect something of the imagery of the substances, it seems to me that the containers should match the ways we use the substances—the way we anoint, for example. This is a subject deserving more discussion than I have room for here, but at least the vessels should be useful for pouring.

A SACRISTY-CHAPEL?

As I pointed out above, near the ambry we need a work station with accommodations for the stock vessels and ancillary vessels, even towels and a sink—but then I'm getting back to the notion of a "liturgical kitchen," yet one that is not only useful but beautiful, a place that feels like common property, like a public place. Which gets me wondering: Is it too far-fetched to imagine this room as a place, a chapel of meditation when it is not busy with use, a "sacristy-chapel" with closets for our holy vessels and vestments and books and other liturgical accoutrements, our oil stocks, our sacred chrism that for us is a sign of the presence of the Holy Spirit, our eucharistic bread and wine that for us is the ultimate sign of the presence of Christ?

12

Thuribles

Gregory Yoshida

In choosing a good thurible, look for the following: stability, insulation and ease of handling. With regard to stability, a censer's base should be heavier than its top. This minimizes the danger of the thurible toppling over and ruining floors, linens or shoes. All good thuribles are also well-insulated to keep most of the heat away from the user. One test method to check for adequate insulation is to feel the bottom of the censer with one piece of burning charcoal in it. If the base is too hot to touch, the interior needs to be lined with additional material, such as a packer of sand wrapped in foil. Also, hold the chain at mid-length when a burning coal is in the censer. If the chain at midpoint is too hot, the thurible cover is probably too thin, the chain is too conducive or the cover is improperly perforated. Look for thuribles with nonmetal knobs or handles that the user pulls open.

Besides metal ones, there are thuribles of pottery as well, mostly without chains, making them good stationary burners. If these bowls are to be carried in procession, they should be relatively light and have comfortable places for hands to securely grip them. Pottery bowls should be lined with sand or gravel to prevent cracking from the heat and to provide insulation from the heat.

How are thuribles best cleaned? For badly soiled metal, the only way is to have a metalworker refurbish it. Otherwise, the traditional method is to boil the entire container and then scrub it to release soot and resin. Be careful

about using chemical compounds, as they may damage metal finishes. When boiling, don't submerge the plastic or wooden knob lest it melt or warp. It is also best to remove the water from the heat source once it's boiling, then submerge the thurible. This avoids metal warping. Be sure to completely dry the censer to prevent rust. If the buildup on a metal thurible is very heavy, I have heard of people freezing it and then chipping off the plaque.

13

Caring for Metalware

Marirose Jelicich

Some of the most important objects used in liturgy are often made of metal: chalices, patens, ciboria, candlesticks and sometimes even the processional cross and the cover for the gospel book. Sterling silver and gold (14 karat or higher) are considered to be "precious" metals. Brass, copper, bronze, nickel, stainless steel and aluminum are considered to be "nonprecious" metals. Properly caring for metal objects requires knowing something about their composition, how to clean and store them, and whom to consult about their value and repair.

Prior to the 1960s, church legislation required that at least the inside of chalices be plated in gold. For the past hundred years or so, it was common for the cup of a chalice or ciborium to be made of sterling silver and the base to be made of a less expensive metal. The whole vessel would then be gold plated and lacquered. To ascertain whether a vessel is sterling, look to see if the word "sterling" is stamped on it. If just the cup

portion is sterling, the word may be stamped somewhere around the rim. If the whole chalice is sterling, it may be stamped on the bottom of the base.

Gold-plated vessels are often lacquered because acidic sweat from human hands and atmospheric conditions in general break down the plating over time. Underneath the lacquer, the gold plating and the base metal will oxidize and darken as time passes, and eventually the lacquer itself will wear off. If the entire vessel is sterling, consider having the remaining lacquer and gold plating stripped off. Depending on the thickness of the lacquer and plating, this can be done rather quickly and inexpensively. It can also be done if the vessel is made of a mixture of sterling silver and some other metal, although an esthetic judgment will have to be made about the appearance of the combined metals. Some people do not like the look of a mixed-metal object, although contemporary vessels are often crafted by an effective marriage of metals. The other option is to have the entire vessel stripped, cleaned and then replated with gold, although this is often not worth the cost and effort if the vessel is beautiful without the plating.

Stripping, polishing and replating require the skills of a professional plater, who will most likely be able to tell you the composition of your metalware and may be able to estimate its value. Another person to consult is a jeweler, who is probably equipped to work with vessels or other objects that have inset precious or semiprecious stones. A hundred years ago it was common to use real amethysts, garnets, aquamarines and other such stones in chalices, ciboria and monstrances; they cost only pennies at the time. Today these stones are considered semiprecious.

If the stone is loose, a jeweler can repair the setting. A jeweler can also help estimate the value of the piece, which is helpful when deciding whether to refurbish or replace an object. Jewelers often offer to strip, polish and replate metalware, too. Sometimes, however, they send such work out to platers, so going directly to a plater is generally more cost efficient.

Wine left in a chalice can pit the metal. The best way to clean metalware is to use hot water, a small amount of a mild soap and a soft cloth. After washing, it is important to dry the object thoroughly with a soft cloth. Never use paper toweling; it will scratch the surface. Silver polish can be used on sterling or silver plate. Again, use a soft cloth. For other metals, polishes are not a good idea, especially if the piece is lacquered. Brass polishes will take the lacquer off in spots and leave the piece mottled.

Such damage often occurs with candlesticks. It is best to presume that mass-produced metalware, especially candlesticks and processional crosses, are lacquered. Dusting them off or occasionally washing them with warm water and mild soap, always with a soft cloth, is all that can be done on site. Metal oxidizes even when lacquered, so lacquered brass will still darken over time. The only way to restore a bright shine is to have a plater strip, buff and reapply lacquer to the piece. The price of such work will be about one quarter of the cost of the item if purchased new.

The best way to store metalware, especially sterling or silver plate, is in bags made of a felt-like material called silver cloth, available at fabric stores for approximately $12 a yard. Bags can be sewn to fit various pieces. Silver cloth slows tarnishing and also protects the piece from scratches. While it isn't necessary to wrap the cups between Masses on Sunday, it is worthwhile to store them in cloth bags during the week. Metalware should be stored in a dry place; sacristans should check sacristy vaults for dampness.

Good metal pieces for liturgy are true community treasures. They should be treated like a family's best china. If a piece becomes too fragile for frequent use, perhaps it can be retired to a parish or diocesan museum, or used on rare occasions but replaced by new pieces so that they can be left to future generations.

14

Blessings for Vessels

Some Christian communities have a tradition of blessing God and giving thanks in ritual for new vessels that have been created to hold the eucharist. This blessing is celebrated just before the vessels are used for the first time. (Other Christian communities consider the first use itself as the act that consecrates the vessels.) Ritually marking the first use of new vessels affords the assembly an opportunity to give thanks to God for the gifts of the artist as well as the art, to remember, as Saint Paul says in the second letter to the Corinthians, that we hold a treasure in earthen vessels, "so that it may be made clear that this extraordinary power belongs to God and does not come from us" (4:7).

This chapter contains rites of blessing for vessels that hold the eucharist from two Christian traditions. The first is from the Roman Catholic *Book of Blessings*. The second is from the *Lutheran Book of Occasional Services*. Neither order presumes the participation of the artists who created the vessels. Yet if it is possible for the artists to participate, perhaps by presenting the vessels at the time of blessing, an important bond could be made between the artists who created the vessels and the community that uses them. The attention lavished on the vessels of the liturgy may, in turn, stir up gratitude in all who participate for the plates and cups of the household table, and lead us all to continually bless the God who fills them with food and drink.

ORDER FOR THE BLESSING OF A CHALICE AND PATEN
(Roman Catholic)

Introduction

1360   The chalice and paten in which wine and bread are offered, consecrated, and received, since they are intended and solely and permanently for the celebration of the eucharist, become "sacred vessels."

1361   The intention, however, of devoting these vessels entirely to the celebration of the eucharist is made manifest before the community by a special blessing which is preferably imparted during Mass.

1362   Any bishop or priest may bless a chalice and paten, provided these have been made according to the norms laid down in the General Instruction of the Roman Missal, nos. 327–34.

1363   If it is a chalice or paten alone that is to be blessed, the text should be suitably adapted.

I. ORDER OF BLESSING WITHIN MASS

1364   In the liturgy of the word, apart from the days listed on the Table of Liturgical Days, nos. 1–9, one or two readings may be taken from those given in no. 1365 below.

Liturgy of the Word

1365   Readings:

1 Corinthians 10:14–22a—Our blessing-cup is a communion with the blood of Christ.

1 Corinthians 11:23–26—This cup is the new covenant in my blood.

Psalm 16:5, 8, 9–10, 11

R. (v. 5) The Lord is my inheritance and my cup.

Psalm 23:1–3a, 3b–4, 5, 6

R. *(v. 5)* You prepare a banquet before me; my cup overflows.

Matthew 20:20–28—You shall indeed drink my cup.

Mark 14:12–16, 22–26—This is my body. This is my blood.

Homily

1366   After the reading of the word of God the homily is given in which the celebrant explains the biblical readings and the meaning of the blessing of a chalice and paten that are used in the celebration of the Lord's Supper.

General Intercessions

1367   The general intercessions follow, either in the form usual at Mass or in the form provided here. The celebrant concludes the intercessions with the prayer of blessing. From the following intentions those best for the occasion may be used or adapted, or other intentions that apply to the particular circumstances may be composed.

The celebrant says:

Let us pray to the Lord Jesus who continuously offers himself for the Church as the bread of life and the cup of salvation. With confidence we make our prayer:

R. Lord, hear our prayer.

Or:

R. Christ Jesus, bread of heavens, grant us eternal life.

Assisting minister:

Savior of all, in obedience to the Father's will, you drank the cup of suffering; grant that we may share in the mystery of your death and thus win the promise of eternal life, and so we pray: **R.**

Assisting minister:

Priest of the most high, hidden yet present in the sacrament of the altar, grant that we may discern by faith what is concealed from our eyes, and so we pray: **R.**

Assisting minister:

Good Shepherd, you give yourself to your disciples as food and drink; grant that, fed by this mystery, we may be transformed into your likeness, and so we pray: **R.**

Assisting minister:

Lamb of God, you commanded your Church to celebrate the paschal mystery under the signs of bread and wine; grant that this memorial may be the summit and source of holiness for all who believe, and so we pray: **R.**

Assisting minister:

Son of God, you wondrously satisfy the hunger and thirst of all who eat and drink at your table; grant that through the mystery of the eucharist we may learn to live your command of love, and so we pray: **R.**

The celebrant then says:

Lord,
by the death and resurrection of your Son
you have brought redemption to the entire world.

Continue in us the work of your grace,
so that, ever recalling the mystery of Christ,
we may finally rejoice at your table in heaven.

Grant this through Christ our Lord.
R. Amen.

Presentation of the Chalice and Paten

1368   When the general intercessions are finished, ministers or representatives of the community that are presenting the chalice and paten place them on the altar. The celebrant then approaches the altar. Meanwhile the following antiphon is sung.

> I will take the cup of salvation and call on the name of the Lord.

Another appropriate song may be sung.

Prayer of Blessing

1369   When the singing is finished, the celebrant says:

> Let us pray.

All pray in silence for a brief period. The celebrant then continues:

> Lord,
>
> with joy we place on your altar
>
> this cup and this paten,
>
> vessels with which we will celebrate
>
> the sacrifice of Christ's new covenant.
>
> May they be sanctified,
>
> for in them the body and blood of Christ
>
> will be offered, consecrated, and received.
>
> Lord,
>
> when we celebrate Christ's faultless sacrifice on earth,
>
> may we be renewed in strength
>
> and filled with your Spirit,
>
> until we join with your saints
>
> at your table in heaven.
>
> Glory and honor be yours for ever and ever.
>
> **R.** Blessed be God for ever.

Preparation of the Altar and Gifts

1370   Afterward the ministers place a corporal on the altar. Some of the congregation bring bread, wine, and water for the celebration of the Lord's sacrifice. The celebrant puts the gifts in the newly blessed paten and chalice and offers them in the usual way. Meanwhile the following antiphon may be sung with Psalm 116:10–19.

> I will take the cup of salvation and offer a sacrifice of praise (alleluia).

Another appropriate song may be sung.

1371   When he has said the prayer "Lord God, we ask you to receive us," the celebrant may incense the gifts and the altar.

1372   If the circumstances of the celebration permit, it is appropriate that the congregation should receive the blood of Christ from the newly blessed chalice.

II. ORDER OF BLESSING WITHIN A CELEBRATION OF THE WORD OF GOD

Introductory Rites

1373   After the people have assembled, the priest, with alb or surplice and stole, goes to the chair. Meanwhile the following antiphon with Psalm 116:10–19 may be sung.

> I will take the cup of salvation and offer a sacrifice of praise (alleluia).

Another appropriate song may be sung.

1374   **The priest greets the people saying:**

> The grace of our Lord Jesus Christ,
> who offered for us his body and blood,
> the love of God,
> and the fellowship of the Holy Spirit
> be with you all.

All reply:

> And also with you.

Other suitable words taken preferably from sacred Scripture may be used.

Introduction

1375   Then the priest briefly addresses the people, preparing them to take part in the celebration and explaining to them the meaning of the rite. He may use these or similar words:

> The celebration of the mystery of the eucharist lies at the center of the Church's life. Christ nourishes and strengthens us with his living body and saving blood that we might be his witnesses in the world. The vessels which hold the bread and wine for the eucharist are treated with reverence and respect for they ultimately will contain the body and blood of the Lord. We ask for God's blessing on these vessels for the holy eucharist and upon us who will be fed from them.

Reading of the Word of God

1376   A reader, another person present, or the priest himself then reads a text of sacred Scripture.

> Brothers and sisters, listen to the words of the first letter of Paul to the Corinthians: *10:14–21*
>
> *Our blessing-cup is a communion with the blood of Christ.*
>
> Therefore, my beloved, avoid idolatry. I am speaking as to sensible people; judge for yourselves what I am saying. The cup of blessing that we bless, is it not a participation in the blood of Christ? The bread that we break, is it not a participation in the body of Christ? Because the loaf of bread is one, we, though many, are one body, for we all partake of the one loaf.
>
> Look at Israel according to the flesh; are not those who eat the sacrifices participants in the altar? So what am I saying? That meat sacrificed to idols is anything? Or that an idol is anything? No, I mean that what they sacrifice, they sacrifice to demons, not to God, and I do not want you to become participants with demons. You cannot drink the cup of the Lord

and also the cup of demons. You cannot partake of the table of the Lord and of the table of demons.

1377   Or:

1 Corinthians 11:23–26 — This cup is the new covenant in my blood.

Matthew 20:20–28 — You shall indeed drink my cup.

Mark 14:12–16, 22–26 — This is my body. This is my blood.

1378   As circumstances suggest, one of the following responsorial psalms may be sung, or some other suitable song, or even a period of silence.

Psalm 16

R. The Lord is my inheritance and my cup.

O LORD, my allotted portion and my cup,

you it is who hold fast my lot. **R.**

I set the LORD ever before me;

with him at my right hand I shall not be disturbed. **R.**

Therefore my heart is glad and my soul rejoices,

my body, too, abides in confidence;

Because you will not abandon my soul to the nether world,

nor will you suffer your faithful one to undergo corruption. **R.**

You will show me the path to life,

fullness of joys in your presence,

the delights at your right hand forever. **R.**

Psalm 23:1–3a, 3b–4, 5, 6
R. *(v. 5)* You prepare a banquet before me; my cup overflows.

1379   After the reading of the word of God the homily is given, in which the priest explains the biblical readings and the meaning of the blessing of a chalice and paten that are used in the celebration of the Lord's Supper.

Presentation of the Chalice and Paten

1380 After the homily the ministers or representatives of the community that are presenting the chalice and paten place them on the altar. The priest then approaches the altar. Meanwhile the following antiphon may be sung.

I will take the cup of salvation and call on the name of the Lord.

Another appropriate song may be sung.

Prayer of Blessing

1381 **The priest says:**

Let us pray.

All pray in silence for a brief period. The priest continues:

Father,

look kindly upon your children,

who have placed on your altar

this cup and this paten.

May these vessels be sanctified + by your blessing,

for with them we will celebrate

the sacrifice of Christ's new covenant.

And may we who celebrate these mysteries on earth

be renewed in strength

and filled with your Spirit

until we join with your saints

at your table in heaven.

Glory and honor be yours for ever and ever.

R. Blessed be God for ever.

Intercessions

1382 The intercessions are then said. The minister introduces them and an assisting ministers or one of those present announces the intentions. From the following those best suited to the occasion may be used or adapted, or other intentions that apply to the particular circumstances may be composed.

The minister says:

Let us pray to the Lord Jesus who continuously offers himself for the Church as the bread of life and the cup of salvation. With confidence we make our prayer:

R. Christ Jesus, bread of heaven, grant us eternal life.

Assisting minister:

Savior of all, in obedience to the Father's will, you drank the cup of suffering; grant that we may share in the mystery of your death and thus win the promise of eternal life, and so we pray: **R.**

Assisting minister:

Priest of the most high, hidden yet present in the sacrament of the altar, grant that we may discern by faith what is concealed from our eyes, and so we pray: **R.**

Assisting minister:

Good Shepherd, you give yourself to your disciples as food and drink; grant that, fed by this mystery, we may be transformed into your likeness, and so we pray: **R.**

Assisting minister:

Lamb of God, you commanded your Church to celebrate the paschal mystery under the signs of bread and wine; grant that this memorial may be the summit and source of holiness for all who believe, and so we pray: **R.**

Assisting minister:

Son of God, you wondrously satisfy the hunger and thirst of all who eat and drink at your table; grant that through the mystery of the eucharist we may learn to live your command of love, and so we pray: **R.**

1383   After the intercessions the priest, in the following or similar words, invites all present to sing or say the Lord's Prayer.

Fastened to the cross, Christ was the way of salvation; in fulfilling the will of the Father he is acclaimed the master of prayer; let his prayer be the source of ours as we say:

All:

Our Father . . .

Concluding Prayer

1384   **The priest then says:**

Lord,
by the death and resurrection of your Son
you have brought redemption to the entire world.

Continue in us the work of your grace,
so that, ever recalling the mystery of Christ,
we may finally rejoice at your table in heaven.

Grant this through Christ our Lord.

R. Amen.

Concluding Rite

1385   **The priest concludes the rite by saying:**

May the Lord, who nourishes us with the body and blood of his Son,
bless and keep you in his love,
now and for ever.

R. Amen.

Then he blesses all present.

> And may almighty God bless you all,
> the Father, and the Son, + and the Holy Spirit.
>
> **R.** Amen.

1386 **Then he dismisses the people, saying:**

> Go in peace.
>
> **R.** Thanks be to God.

1387 It is preferable to end the celebration with a suitable song.

DEDICATION OF WORSHIP FURNISHINGS
(Evangelical Lutheran Church in America)

1 The dedication of worship furnishings is set within the liturgy for Holy Communion. This prayer, with the appropriate petition, is said following the presentation of the gifts and prior to the offertory prayer.

2 The worship furnishing may be brought forward with the gifts, or, where that is not possible, the minister may say the prayer from the location of the furnishing being dedicated.

3 Prayers for the dedication of a baptismal font and an altar are included in the order for Dedication (of a church building).

4 When circumstances suggest a longer form of dedication, the appropriate petition below may replace the alternatives in the General Order of Blessing.

Stand

5 **The prayer is said.**

> Let us pray.
> Blessed are you, O Lord our God, king of the universe.
> You have enriched our lives with every good and perfect gift;
> you have commanded us to show your splendor to our children
> and to praise you with lives of love, justice, and joy.

(Paten/chalice)

Accept this *paten/chalice* which we offer in thanksgiving;
may all who receive the heavenly *food and drink* be sustained
by your grace and power.

Or:

Accept this _____ which we offer in thanksgiving;
may those who use it do so in reverence and in love,
giving honor and glory to your holy name.

The prayer concludes:

Bring us all at length to your perfect kingdom,
where you live and reign with the Son and the Holy Spirit,
now and forever. Amen.

The service continues with the offertory prayer.

GENERAL ORDER OF BLESSING
(Evangelical Lutheran Church in America)

1   Care should be exercised to make certain that God's blessing may properly be asked upon the object, place or event under consideration.

2   This order of blessing may be augmented with hymns, the Lord's Prayer or other prayers, and a procession.

3   When the congregation has assembled at the place of blessing:

Presider: Brothers and sisters in Christ: Today we seek God's blessing as we gather with thankfulness to *bless/dedicate* this _____ to the glory of God.

4   A psalm or canticle may follow.

5   One or more lessons from the Bible may be read.

6   A hymn may be sung.

7   The prayers are said:

Presider: All your works praise you, O Lord,
All: and your faithful servants bless you.

Presider:

Blessed are you, O Lord our God, king of the universe.
You made the whole earth for your glory;
all creation praises you.
We lift our voices to join the songs of heaven and earth,
of things seen and unseen.

You stretched out the heavens like a curtain;
you divided the day from the night;
you appointed times and seasons for work and for rest,
    for tearing down and building up.
You blessed your people through all generations
    and guided them in life and death:
    Abraham and Sarah;
    Moses and Miriam;
    Isaiah and all the prophets;
    Mary, mother of our Lord;
    Peter, James, John,
    and all the apostles;
    and all the saints and witnesses
    in your Church of ages past,
    in whom your Spirit spoke and moved.

One of the following or another appropriate prayer is said:

Be with us now and bless us
as we *set apart/dedicate* this _____ to your glory and praise.
Grant us faith to know your gracious purpose in all things,
give us joy in them,
and lead us to the building up of your kingdom;
through your Son, Jesus Christ our Lord,

who lives and reigns with you and the Holy Spirit,
one God, now and forever.
Amen.

Or:

Accept this *paten/chalice* which we offer in thanksgiving;
may all who receive the heavenly *food and drink* be sustained
by your grace and power.

Or:

Accept this _____ which we offer in thanksgiving;
may those who use it do so in reverence and love,
giving honor and glory to your holy name.

The service concludes:

Presider: Let us bless the Lord.
All: Thanks be to God.

Presider: The blessing of almighty God, the Father, the + Son,
and the Holy Spirit, be with you all.
All: Amen.

15

Noble, Simple, Worthy and Beautiful

NOBLE BEAUTY

The fine arts are deservedly ranked among the noblest activities of human genius, and this applies especially to religious art and to its highest achievement, sacred art. These arts, by their very nature, are oriented toward the infinite beauty of God, which they attempt in some way to portray by the work of human hands. They are dedicated to advancing God's praise and glory to the degree that they center on the single aim of turning the human spirit devoutly toward God.

The Church has therefore always been the friend of the fine arts, has ever sought their noble help, and has trained artists with the special aim that all things set apart for use in divine worship are truly worthy, becoming, and beautiful, signs and symbols of the supernatural world. The Church has always regarded itself as the rightful arbiter of the arts, deciding which of the works of artists are in accordance with faith, with reverence, and with honored traditional laws and are thereby suited for sacred use.

The Church has been particularly careful to see that sacred furnishings worthily and beautifully serve the dignity of worship and has admitted changes in materials, design, or ornamentation prompted by the progress of the technical arts with the passage of time.

Wherefore it has pleased the Fathers to issue the following decrees on these matters.

The Church has not adopted any particular style of art as its very own but has admitted styles from every period, according to the proper genius and circumstances of peoples and the requirements of the many different rites in the Church. Thus, in the course of the centuries, the Church has brought into being a treasury of art that must be very carefully preserved. The art of our own days coming from every race and region, shall also be given free scope in the Church, on condition that it serves the places of worship and sacred rites with the reverence and honor due to them. In this way contemporary art can add its own voice to that wonderful chorus of praise sung by the great masters of past ages of Catholic faith.

In encouraging and favoring art that is truly sacred, Ordinaries should strive after noble beauty rather than mere sumptuous display. This principle is to apply also in the matter of sacred vestments and appointments.

Let bishops carefully remove from the house of God and from other places of worship those works of artists that are repugnant to faith and morals and to Christian devotion and that offend true religious sense either by their grotesqueness or by the deficiency, mediocrity, or sham in their artistic quality.

When churches are to be built, let great care be taken that they are well suited to celebrating liturgical services and to bringing about the active participation of the faithful. . . .

When deciding on works of art, local Ordinaries shall give hearing to the diocesan commission on sacred art, and if need be, to others who are especially expert, as well as to the commissions referred to in an art. 44, 45, and 46. Ordinaries must be very careful to see that sacred furnishings and valuable works of art are not disposed of or damaged, for they are the adornment of the house of God.

Bishops should have a special concern for artists, so as to imbue them with the spirit of sacred art and liturgy. This they may do in person or through competent priests who are gifted with a knowledge and love of art.

It is also recommended that schools or academies of sacred art to train artists be founded in those parts of the world where they seem useful.

All artists who, prompted by their talents, desire to serve God's glory in holy Church, should ever bear in mind that they are engaged in a kind of sacred imitation of God the Creator and are concerned with works intended to be used in Catholic worship, to uplift the faithful, and to foster their devotion and religious formation.

Along with the revision of the liturgical books, as laid down in art. 25, there is to be an early revision of the canons and ecclesiastical statutes regulating the supplying of material things involved in sacred worship. This applies in particular to the worthy and well-planned construction of places of worship, the design and construction of altars, the nobility, placement, and security of the eucharistic tabernacle, the practicality and dignity of the baptistry, the appropriate arrangement of sacred images and church decoration and appointments. Laws that seem less suited to the reformed liturgy are to be brought into harmony with it or else abolished; laws that are helpful are to be retained if already in use or introduced where they are lacking.

With art. 22 of this Constitution as the norm, the territorial bodies of bishops are empowered to make adaptations to the needs and customs of their different regions; this applies especially to the material and design of sacred furnishings and vestments.

Constitution on the Sacred Liturgy Sacrosanctum concilium *(1964),*
122–24, 126–28

LITURGICAL VESSELS

Among the requisites for the celebration of Mass, the sacred vessels hold a place of honor, especially the chalice and paten, which are used in presenting, consecrating, and receiving the bread and wine.

Vessels should be made from materials that are solid and that in the particular region are regarded as noble. The conference of bishops will be the judge in this matter. But preference is to be given to materials that do not break easily or become unusable.

Chalices and other vessels that serve as receptacles for the blood of the Lord are to have a cup of nonabsorbent material. The base may be of any other solid and worthy material.

Vessels that serve as receptacles for the eucharistic bread, such as a paten, ciborium, pyx, monstrance, etc., may be made of other materials that are prized in the region, for example, ebony or other hard woods, as long as they are suited to sacred use.

For the consecration of hosts one rather large paten may properly be used; on it is placed the bread for the priest as well as for the ministers and the faithful.

Vessels made from metal should ordinarily be gilded on the inside if the metal is one that rusts; gilding is not necessary if the metal is more precious than gold and does not rust.

The artist may fashion the sacred vessels in a shape that is in keeping with the culture of each region, provided each type of vessel is suited to the intended liturgical use.

For the blessing or consecration of vessels the rites prescribed in the liturgical books are to be followed.

General Instruction of the Roman Missal, *289–96*

NO LACK OF ARTISTIC STYLE

Particular respect and care are due to the sacred vessels, both the chalice and paten for the celebration of the eucharist, and the ciboria for the communion of the faithful. The form of the vessels must be appropriate for the liturgical use for which they are meant. The material must be noble, durable, and in every case adapted to sacred use. In this sphere, judgment belongs to the episcopal conference of the individual regions. Use is not to be made of simple baskets or other recipients meant for ordinary use outside the sacred celebrations, nor are the sacred vessels to be of poor quality or lacking any artistic style. Before being used, chalices and patens must be blessed by the bishop or by a priest.

Inaestimabile donum *(1980), 16*

16

The Material of Liturgical Vessels

LITURGICAL LAW APPLIED

Frederick R. McManus

The directives for the appropriate materials of liturgical or ritual vessels, called *vasa sacra* in Latin, are a clear and distinct area of church law. It is a secondary area but important enough. The vessels are chiefly plates or dishes commonly called patens and ciboria (singular, ciborium), small containers with attached covers called pyxes (singular, pyx) for the eucharistic bread, and cups or chalices for drinking the consecrated wine. These vessels that hold the body and blood of Christ have rich histories of use and design. Diverse norms and rules have affected their development as functional works of art for ritual use. And they constitute a simple illustration of the liturgical law of the Roman rite in practice.

TEXT AND CONTEXT

Current law regarding liturgical vessels is rooted in the 1963 Constitution on the Sacred Liturgy *Sacrosanctum concilium* (SC), enacted by the Church's supreme authority, the Second Vatican Council (1963–65). The constitution decrees,

> Along with the revision of the liturgical books . . . there is to be an early revision of the canons and ecclesiastical statutes regulating the supplying of material [external] things involved in sacred worship. . . . [T]he territorial bodies of bishops are empowered to make adaptations to the needs and customs of their different regions; this applies especially to the material and design of sacred furnishings and vestments. (SC, 128)

The issues are thus two: first, general liturgical reform of the Roman rite of the Latin or Western church; second, subsidiarity in church governance, hence the immediate role of national or regional conferences of bishops. To understand or explain any example of canon or church law, however, not only the words of the text (or the words in which an unwritten custom may be articulated) must be studied, but also the all-important context (see canon 17).

The surrounding context of these prescriptions is found in the same seventh chapter of SC, in particular its opening exposition: The church is "the friend of the fine arts," with the aim that "all things set apart for use in divine worship are truly worthy, becoming, and beautiful, signs and symbols of the supernatural world" (#122). This is offered as the rationale for the church's right to pass judgment on the arts, albeit with a fundamental openness to development, specifically in regard to church furnishings—including both the form and material of liturgical vessels. The paragraph of introductory context reads: "The Church has been particularly careful to see that sacred furnishings worthily and beautifully serve the dignity of worship and has admitted changes in materials, design, and ornamentation prompted by the progress of the technical arts with the passage of time" (#122). Today that seventh chapter and indeed the whole constitution should be read and reread.

SC affirms the importance and dignity of what we now have come to call "the environment of worship" under an all-embracing norm of simplicity: Bishops and other ordinaries, "by the encouragement and favor they show to art which is truly sacred, should strive after noble beauty rather than mere sumptuous display *[potius nobilem intendant pulchritudinem quam meram sumptuositatem]*. This principle is to apply also in the matter of sacred vestments and ornaments" (#124). It is also an application of other analogous, overriding decisions of the general council in matters of worship: "In this reform, both texts and rites should be so drawn up that they express more clearly the holy things they signify" (#21); "[t]he rites should be marked by a noble simplicity" (#34).

In the United States, the principle of subsidiarity—fostered by the great council along with collegiality and later a formal goal for the 1983 Latin church's *Code of Canon Law*—was soon carried out in regard to the materials for liturgical vessels. In November 1969 the U.S. National Conference of Catholic Bishops, in full accord with Vatican II, enacted a decree that is still in effect: "Materials other than the traditional ones may be used for sacred furnishings, provided they are suitable for liturgical use, subject to the further judgment of the local ordinary in doubtful cases" (Appendix to the *General Instruction of the Roman Missal* for the Dioceses of the United States, 288). Given the size and diversity of this country, the decision to open the door and, as it were, to transfer any question to local judgment (whether parochial or diocesan) was appropriate enough and has worked out in practice ever since.

STATUTES

What then were the revisions of "canons and ecclesiastical statutes" promised by Vatican II in the radical liturgical reform as this affected the material of liturgical vessels? The primary source for reformed church law on the matter is the 1970 *General Instruction of the Roman Missal* (GIRM). In the usual style it is both expository and then normative; it is church regulation, always with the understanding that the least law is the best law. The GIRM was revised in 1975 and again in 2000, but little changed in the law concerning vessels, so we will examine here the 1970 text.

The pertinent section of GIRM is headed "Requisites for Celebrating Mass," under the subhead "Sacred Vessels." Such vessels "hold a place of honor, especially the chalice and paten, which are used in presenting, consecrating, and receiving the bread and wine" (GIRM, 289). Six rules follow (with emphasis added to the words of principal significance):

290. Vessels should be made from *materials that are solid* and that in the particular region are *regarded as noble*. The conference of bishops will be the judge in

this matter. But *preference [praeferantur]* is to be given to materials that *do not break easily or become unusable.* [See also 2000 GIRM, 329.]

291. Chalices and other vessels that serve as receptacles for the blood of the Lord are to have a *cup of nonabsorbent material.* The base may be of any other solid and worthy material. [See also 2000 GIRM, 330.]

292. Vessels that serve as receptacles for the eucharistic bread, such as a paten, ciborium, pyx, monstrance, etc., may be made of other materials that are prized in the region, for example, ebony or other hard *[durioribus]* woods, as long as they are suited to sacred use. [See also 2000 GIRM, 329.]

293. For the consecration of hosts *one rather large paten* may properly be used; on it is placed the bread for the priest as well as for the ministers and the faithful. [See also 2000 GIRM, 331.]

294. Vessels made from metal should *ordinarily [plerumque]* be gilded on the inside if the metal is one that rusts; gilding is not necessary if the metal is precious and does not rust. [See also 2000 GIRM, 328.]

295. The artist may fashion the sacred vessels in a shape that is in keeping with the culture of each region, provided that each type of vessel is suited to the intended liturgical use. [See also 2000 GIRM, 332.]

ONE LOAF, ONE CUP

Of these six articles two are not specifically related to the materials of vessels. Rather, they speak of the form or style, the design: One article speaks of larger plates, dishes, patens for the consecrated bread (see #293); the other leaves to the free discretion of artists or craftspersons fresh designs for vessels, always suited to their liturgical use but also in harmony with various, diverse religious and artistic cultures (see #295).

On the first point, attention must now be paid to the biblical concept of "one loaf" for the eucharist to be shared by the whole community, which thus probably requires a plate or dish that is a good deal larger than has been common in the past. The same principle apples to the "one cup" to be shared, with a larger cup needed now that communion under both kinds has been restored to the church in accord with the divine injunction. If all communicants cannot literally partake from one cup, other cups are used, too. But the wine is consecrated in one cup and one flagon, with the flagon's contents being poured into other cups at the fraction rite of the Mass.

What is obvious is that the form of vessels will often enough influence the choice of materials in which they are executed. What is more important is the openness, flexibility and freedom now available in canon law.

The law now makes reasonable, even nonrestrictive, demands. First, materials should be *solid* and, by "preference," *not easily broken or breakable;* the chief test, however, is that they be "noble" according to the cultural or esthetic standards of the region (see #290). The statement, open and encouraging to creative choices, applies to all vessels. It has been imaginatively employed, in full conformity to conciliar intentions embraced in the liturgy constitution, in the use of woods and nonmetallic materials such as glass, heavy crystal, substantial ceramics, and the like. Judgments about artistic quality are not easy; they should be left to artists and artisans of repute and to liturgical committees and commissions. What the law properly demands is solidity and the avoidance of any material that is delicate—surely not a problem in the creative productions of the post-conciliar period.

Next, a special expectation of eucharistic cups or chalices is added: The material of the cup area may not be such that it absorbs liquid—a clear enough prescription, easily satisfied whether metal, hardwood, glass, ceramic, or the like is chosen. Should a material that is possibly absorbent be used, its interior may be carefully coated or lined to avoid any such problem. Finally, if a cup for the eucharist is designed with a foot or base, as has been usual but is no longer specifically demanded, the material may be freely chosen, always provided it meets the requirements of worthiness and solidity (see #291).

In turn the various kinds of vessels used to contain the consecrated bread or host(s), whether during the celebration of eucharist or for reservation or exposition, are mentioned, but only to open the door as widely as possible to diversity of materials. The demands are the same: suitability (in quality and function) and solidity. In particular, examples are given: ebony (a hardwood, highly regarded in some places) and the more durable woods (see #292). It is evident that other examples may be added to this proposal, including solid glass and the like. As is also evident, the material need not be nonabsorbent, as is expected with cups for liquid.

Article 294 deals with a problem that is now largely past. It was once expected that liturgical vessels be almost always metallic and indeed made of precious metals or at least gilded. Now, if a metal that is likely to rust or be subject to similar corrosion is used, the interior should ordinarily (*plerumque*, "in most cases") be gilded; otherwise not (see #294).

As already suggested, the chief characteristic of the revised norms is that materials for vessels should be chosen most freely for their beauty and elegance, with the proviso that they are also solid and generally unbreakable.

THE NEW GIRM

As explained above, the recent revision (in the year 2000) of the GIRM changed little in the law regarding vessels. As this book goes to press, an official English translation of the revised GIRM is not yet available, so here is a summary of the changes. The pertinent law is found in articles 327–34 of the 2000 edition of the GIRM.

The first article, 327, points out that among the material objects used in liturgy, the vessels hold a place of honor. Articles 333 and 334 are also new: The former reminds us that the rite of blessing of vessels from the Roman ritual should be used prior to the vessels being used, and the latter reminds architects to provide a sacrarium—a special sink that drains into the earth rather than a sewer—for the cleansing of vessels.

The other articles reorder what was originally prescribed in the 1970 GIRM, as indicated in the brackets accompanying the quotes above. One new norm is introduced in 2000 GIRM, 332 (1970 GIRM, 295): Liturgical vessels should be distinguishable from everyday tableware. This does not mean that glass vessels or baskets are *de facto* excluded. Depending on the parish, fine crystal chalices (say, ten inches tall) or handmade ceremonial baskets (say, from Africa or South America) are not among those designed for everyday use, nor are they used in people's homes. The aim of this principle is to prevent one from running over to the rectory dining room for extra wine glasses instead of providing for the liturgy what the liturgy requires.

BASKETS

How canon law regarding liturgical vessels should be interpreted in the Christian community involves an even broader reflection. But first another ecclesiastical document should also be cited.

In the spring of 1980 the competent Roman department issued an instruction with some norms related to the eucharistic mystery; it goes by the name *Inaestimabile donum*. Canonically and technically, the instruction was and is not a law *(lex)* or general decree (see canon 34). Thus it differs from GIRM, which is part of an official liturgical book (the *Roman Missal*)—duly promulgated and containing the liturgical law now in force (see canon 2). A canonical instruction, however important and useful, is not a law and may not change or abrogate a law. (Although called for convenience an "instruction," the *General Instruction of the Roman Missal* is technically something quite different, namely, an *institutio generalis*.)

The 1980 document is largely cautionary in dealing with liturgical developments, but it carefully avoids anything that might be construed as changing the existing liturgical law. A paragraph on materials of liturgical vessels repeats the existing norms in summary fashion:

> Special honor and care are due to sacred vessels, whether the chalice and paten suitable for the eucharistic celebration or pyxes [ciboria] to be used for holy communion. The form of sacred vessels intended for liturgical use, however, is to be suitable *[idonea sit oportet]*, the material to be noble, durable, and always accommodated to sacred use. It is for the episcopal conference of the region to judge this matter. (*Inaestimabile donum*, 16)

The only new issue follows: "It is not lawful to use very simple baskets *[simplicia canistra]* or others intended for common use outside sacred celebrations or those which are of poorer quality or lack all artistry" (#16). Some people characterize this instruction as regressive, and perhaps this is true of other sections of the document or of its tone overall. But article 16 is not regressive but understandably cautionary: Certain kinds of baskets, used commonly as containers for bread at table, may sometimes be unworthy or unfitting in style or material, for example, if they are mean or tawdry and fit the 1980 document's cautious definition of exclusion. This is most likely rare. Some and probably most baskets may be elegant and graceful enough, and they may enhance the authentic sign of the one loaf of bread to become the body of Christ.

Clearly baskets of metal or ceramic or the like are not excluded: one may find examples of highest artistry even in museums. Similarly, baskets of wicker or other wooden materials may just as easily possess considerable quality of design and material—hardly of poor or common level, or notably simple in ordinary estimation. They should be sufficiently solid rather than fragile; if open in their design, for example, they may need a linen or other cloth lining such as is often used with baskets for bread.

FLEXIBILITY FOR CREATIVITY

This may seem like a needless and fussy excursus, but it has its own point: The Roman texts are at least extremely open and reasonable if examined with any care. This is what is meant by "interpretation in text" (see canon 17). And thus we return to what was said in the beginning about understanding a law in its context as well. The context may be the immediate one or it may be much wider. The concept of canonical context has been enlarged and greatly strengthened in recent years by commentators of major reputation, by Ladislas Örsy (Catholic University of America) in general, and by John Huels (St. Paul University, Ottawa) in liturgical law. Add to this the guiding goals of canonical revision from 1959 to 1983, both pastoral concerns and subsidiarity, and every trace of rigidity disappears or should disappear.

A final note may help to explain how limited in scope the canon law, which includes the liturgical law as a subset or species, has to be in matters artistic. Most directives of this kind must be general, often in the style of exhortation to artistic quality. If negative or prohibitory, they have to be few and specific.

An analogy to questions of design and material of church furnishings can be seen in liturgical music, sometimes called sacred music in distinction to religious music. There is little that can be achieved canonically or juridically to enhance or raise the level of the music of worship. The law could perhaps exclude music deemed "unworthy," like the bizarre or grotesque, music that is lewd by association, or culturally unacceptable song. Perhaps in a more positive fashion, the law could encourage quality in liturgical music by exhortation, educational demands, and the like. Yet it is unrealistic to expect that regulations and norms can achieve great advances in what may often be matters of subjective musical taste—or, in the present case, judgments of quality in the materials acceptable for liturgical or ritual use.

Thus it is repeatedly necessary to resort to broad concepts of nobility, simplicity and authenticity of purpose in opposition to the tawdry or stereotypical. The materials and design of liturgical vessels are now supported by the free and open norms of the liturgical law, with few prohibitions needed and with generous flexibility and creativity invited.

About the Artists and Authors

Margaret Fischer is an enamelist and metalsmith who lives in Shaker Heights, Ohio. She teaches in the art studios at Case Western Reserve University and works in the Office for Pastoral Liturgy of the Roman Catholic Diocese of Cleveland.

Edward Foley, Capuchin, is professor of liturgy and music at the Catholic Theological Union in Chicago. He holds a doctorate in liturgical studies from the University of Notre Dame.

William Frederick, professional metalsmith, specializes in the design and execution of custom presentation pieces in gold, silver and other metals, including chalices and other religious objects, jewelry and silverware for home and professional use. He lives and hammers on the north side of Chicago.

Mark Humenick is a metalsmith who lives and works in Santa Fe, New Mexico. He subscribes to this notion from Walter Gropius's 1919 Bauhaus Manifesto: "The artist is a craftsman of heightened awareness."

Marirose Jelicich has created award-winning vessels for use in the liturgy for more than 15 years, yet she has not lost her wonder or joy in translating a client's spiritual vision into a vessel for celebration. Her studio is in Sacramento, California.

Frederick R. McManus, a presbyter of the archdiocese of Boston and a pioneer of the twentieth-century liturgical movement in the United States, teaches at the Catholic University of America in Washington, D.C., and is a canon law consultant for the Bishop's Committee on the Liturgy of the U.S. National Conference of Catholic Bishops.

Peter Mazar is the author of *To Crown the Year: Decorating the Church through the Seasons* (Chicago: LTP, 1995) and *School Year, Church Year: Customs and Decorations for the Classroom* (Chicago: LTP, 2001).

G. Thomas Ryan is the author of *The Sacristy Manual* (Chicago: LTP, 1992) and a liturgical design consultant in Massachusetts.

Gregory Yoshida is a teacher and maker of incense in Monterey Park, California.

Photo Credits

Shown on the cover is Sarah Hall's *Chalice and Paten for a Small Community*, reverse-painted with gold leaf. A 24-karat gold wheat pattern spirals out from the center of the paten. The chalice is 9" high and the paten 14" in diameter, and were created for Peter Larisey, SJ, by Toronto glass artist Sarah Hall. It won a Bene Award for outstanding liturgical art in 1993.

Most of the photos in this book are identified with captions and were provided by the artists in whose portfolio section the photos occur. The photo on page 9 is of a mouth-blown chalice by Jeff Ulrich of Colorado, as is the photo of the flagon and chalice on page 15. The illustrations on pages 10, 11, 12 and 13 are by Robin Faulkner Simunek. The chalices pictured on page 16 are by Joseph Aspell, SM. Photo courtesy of Joseph Aspell. The photo on page 19 shows the credence table at the Cathedral of the Assumption, Louisville, Kentucky, and is by David Philippart. The photo on page 20 is the same as the cover and is by Sarah Hall. The photo on page 35 is by Tina Neff. The photo on page 79 is of the ambry in St. Patrick Church, Merced, California, designed by Armando Ruiz with vessels by Bruce Freund. Photo by Armando Ruiz. The photo on page 81 is of the ambry in Magnificat Chapel, Villa Maria, Pennsylvania, designed by Richard Podulka. Photo © 1995 by Peter Renerts. Used with permission. The photo on page 82 is of vessels by Bruce Freund for St. Patrick Church, San Diego, California. Photo by Armando Ruiz. The photo on page 83 is a close-up of the vessels in the ambry on page 79. Photo by Armando Ruiz. The photo on page 84 is of the ambry in St. David the King Church, Princeton Junction, New Jersey, designed by Peter E. Smith. Photo by Peter E. Smith. The photo on page 85 is of the ambry in Most Holy Trinity Church, Saco, Maine, designed by Rita Schiltz, OP, and Barbara Chenicek, OP. Photo by Brian Vander Brink. The photo on page 87 is of the thurible for St. Peter Church, Cleveland, Ohio, made by Diane Pinchot, OSU. Photo by Eileen Crowley Horak. The photo at the top of page 88 is by Tim Stempniewski. The photos of thuribles at the lower left of page 88 and on page 89 are provided by Adam Kochlin designs. Both thuribles are by potter Richard Reuter. The photo on page 91 is of the sterling chalice with appliqué design made by William Frederick for Reverend Michael Perko of Loyola University, Chicago.